PELICAN BOOKS

SPINOZA

Stuart Hampshire was born in 1914. He was educated at Balliol College, Oxford, and was elected a Fellow of All Souls College in 1936. He was a tutor in philosophy until the war, when he served in the Army. After a short period in the Foreign Office, he returned to the teaching of philosophy at University College, London, in 1947. In 1950 he became a Fellow of New College, Oxford. From 1960–63 he was Grote Professor of Philosophy of Mind and Logic at University College, London. In 1963 he was appointed Professor of Philosophy at Princeton University

He is the author of *Thought and Action* and *Freedom and the Individual,* and of articles in philosophical journals.

STUART HAMPSHIRE

Spinoza

PENGUIN BOOKS

Penguin Books Ltd, Harmondsworth, Middlesex, England
Penguin Books Inc., 7110 Ambassador Road, Baltimore, Maryland 21207, U.S.A.
Penguin Books Australia Ltd, Ringwood, Victoria, Australia

—

First published 1951
Reprinted 1953
Reprinted with revisions 1962
Reprinted 1965, 1967, 1970

—

Copyright © Stuart Hampshire, 1951

Printed in the United States of America
Set in Monotype Fournier

CONTENTS

EDITORIAL FOREWORD   7

PREFACE   9

I   *Philosophical Background*   11

II   *Outline of Metaphysics*   30

III   *Knowledge and Intellect*   82

IV   *Freedom and Morality*   121

V   *Politics and Religion*   177

VI   *The Nature of Metaphysics*   210

APPENDIX: *Life*   227

INDEX   236

To B.

Editorial Foreword

Professor Stuart Hampshire's study of the philosophy of Spinoza is one of a series of philosophical works which are to appear in a similar form. In the main this series is devoted to the history of philosophy; it will contain original studies of the work of a number of outstanding philosophers from Plato to Peirce; but it is also to include books on more general topics, such as logic, the theory of knowledge, political philosophy, ethics and the philosophy of science.

The series is not intended to reflect the standpoint, or advance the views, of any one philosophical school. Each contributor has been left free to handle his chosen subject in his own way. Where the subject, as in this case, is a particular philosopher, the aim has been to give such a critical exposition of his most important doctrines as will be intelligible and interesting even to the non-specialist without any sacrifice of accuracy or completeness: so far as possible to abstain from technical jargon, but also to avoid undue simplification.

In the case of a philosopher like Spinoza, this end is not easy to attain. Even in Professor Hampshire's most lucid exposition of it, Spinoza's thought is sometimes hard to follow. Spinoza's arguments are subtle and the questions with which he deals as difficult as they are important. But the intrinsic, as well as the historical, interest of his philosophy fully justifies the intellectual effort that is required to master it. It is to those who are willing to make this effort, whether or not they be professional philosophers, that Professor Hampshire's book is addressed.

A. J. Ayer

Preface

THE standard edition of the works of Spinoza in Latin is that of Dr Carl Gebhardt (Heidelberg, 1925); a more widely available edition is that of Van Vloten and Land in two volumes (The Hague, 1882).

English translations of the *Ethics* and of *The Treatise on the Correction of the Understanding* have appeared in Everyman's Library and in the Bohn Series; the two-volume edition of the *Chief Works of Spinoza* in the Bohn Series also includes translations of the *Theological-Political Treatise* and of the *Political Treatise*. There is an earlier and better translation of the *Ethics* and *On the Correction of the Understanding* by W. Hale White (better known as 'Mark Rutherford') and Amelia S. Stirling.

The best English edition of the *Letters*, which are indispensable for an understanding of Spinoza, is *The Correspondence of Spinoza* edited by A. Wolf (Allen and Unwin, 1929), which has a useful introduction and notes.

The early *Principles of Descartes' Philosophy*, with its appendix, the *Metaphysical Thoughts*, is of importance chiefly to those studying the development of Spinoza's thought and writing. The early *Short Treatise on God, Man, and his Well-being was* translated and annotated by Professor A. Wolf; the *Short Treatise* is also primarily of interest to students of Spinoza's development.

The most careful studies of Spinoza in English are *A Study of Spinoza's Ethics* by H. H. Joachim (Oxford University Press, 1901) and the posthumously published lectures, *Spinoza's*

Tractatus De Intellectus Emendatione: A Commentary (Oxford University Press, 1940), by the same author: also *The Philosophy of Spinoza* by H. A. Wolfson (Harvard University Press, 1934). The following will also be found useful: *Spinoza: His Life and Philosophy* by Sir Frederick Pollock (Duckworth, 1880), *Spinoza, Descartes and Maimonides* by L. Roth (Oxford University Press, 1924), *Spinoza* by L. Roth (Benn, 1929), *Spinoza's Theory of Knowledge* by G. H. R. Parkinson (Oxford University Press, 1954), and the *Political Works*, edited and translated by A. C. Wernham (Oxford University Press, 1958).

More advanced students will find some articles of great value in the *Chronicon Spinozanum* issued in The Hague as the organ of the Societas Spinozana.

All references to the *Ethics* are to the originally numbered Parts and Propositions, Definitions, Demonstrations, and Notes of that work; all such references appear in brackets in the text in abbreviated form, e.g. '*Ethics Part* II. *Proposition* XIV and *Demonstration*'. (*Ethics Pt.* II. *Prop.* XIV and *Dem.*) References to the *Letters* follow the numeration of Wolf's English edition. The versions given follow the existing translations with a few minor alterations.

I am grateful to Mrs Martha Kneale and to the Editor of the series for valuable suggestions.

CHAPTER ONE

Philosophical Background

'I DO not presume to have discovered the best philosophy', Spinoza wrote (*Letter* LXXVI), 'but I know
that I understand the true one.' Spinoza is the most ambi-
tious and uncompromising of all modern philosophers, and
it is partly for this reason that he is supremely worth
studying. He exhibits the metaphysical mind and temdera-
ment at its purest and most intense; he is the perfect example of the pure philosopher. No other modern philosopher
of equal stature has made such exalted claims for philosophy, or had such a clear vision of the scope and range of
pure philosophical thinking. He conceived it to be the function of the philosopher to render the universe as a whole
intelligible, and to explain man's place within the universe;
he devoted his whole life to the execution of this design,
and he was confident that he had finally succeeded, at least
in general outline. The only instrument which he allowed
himself, or thought necessary to his purpose, was his own
power of logical reasoning; at no point does he appeal to
authority or revelation or common consent; nor does he
anywhere rely on literary artifice or try to reinforce rational
argument by indirect appeals to emotion. No one, however
sceptical of the value of metaphysical systems, can fail to
be impressed by the magnitude of his design; and in

proportion as one is rationally and not dogmatically sceptical about the limits of human reason, one cannot neglect to probe into the execution of his design. Spinoza is the test case for those who reject deductive metaphysics; he makes almost every claim which has ever been made for philosophy and for the power of pure reason, and within his system tries to substantiate these claims. Those who are concerned to delimit the scope of pure philosophical thinking cannot anywhere in western philosophy, at least since Plato, find all the traditional pretensions of metaphysics more clearly exemplified than they are in Spinoza.

A philosopher has always been thought of as someone who tries to achieve a complete view of the universe as a whole, and of man's place in the universe; he has traditionally been expected to answer those questions about the design and purpose of the universe, and of human life, which the various special sciences do not claim to answer; philosophers have generally been conceived as unusually wise or all-comprehending men whose systems are answers to those large, vague questions about the purpose of human existence which present themselves to most people at some period of their lives. Spinoza fulfils all these expectations. Within his system almost every major and recurring metaphysical and moral issue is answered, and is answered definitely and without evasion. For Spinoza philosophy was not merely one useful or necessary intellectual discipline among others, or somehow ancillary to the special sciences; it was the only complete and essential form of knowledge, in relation to which all other inquiries are partial and subordinate. Like Plato and most other great metaphysicians, he thought of philosophy as the pursuit of wisdom and of the knowledge of the right way of life; only in so far as we understand true philosophy can we know how we ought to live, and know also what kind of scientific and other knowledge is useful and attainable. It follows that philosophy must be the essential foundation of all other inquiries, none of which are to be thought of as being on the same level as the master-inquiry. He begins his fragment *On the Correction of the Understanding*, which is an essay on the theory of knowledge, with a magnificent personal statement, which summarizes the classical approach to philosophy, descending ultimately from Plato.

'After experience had taught me that all things which are ordinarily encountered in common life are vain and futile, and when I saw that all things which were the occasions and objects of my fears had in themselves nothing of good or evil except in so far as the mind was moved by them; I at length determined to inquire if there were anything which was a true good, capable of imparting itself, by which alone the mind could be affected to the exclusion of all else; whether indeed anything existed by the discovery and acquisition of which I might be put in possession of a joy continuous and supreme to all eternity.' ... True philosophy is the discovery of the 'true good', and without knowledge of the true good human happiness is impossible. So philosophy is a matter of supreme practical urgency, not simply the gratification of an intellectual or theoretical interest. The order of Spinoza's thought and the whole structure of his philosophy cannot be understood unless they are seen as culminating in his doctrine of human freedom and happiness and in his prescription of the right way of life.

Such an exalted and extensive conception of the scope of philosophy has only gradually within the last hundred years come to seem unfamiliar and in need of special explanation; among Spinoza's philosophical contemporaries in the seventeenth century such claims were normal, although not unchallenged. With the growth of modern science and the consequent increasing specialization of knowledge, the word 'philosophy' has gradually changed its meaning. In this century philosophy is no longer generally thought of as a kind of super-science to which all the special sciences are subordinate and contributory; as the experimental methods of the modern scientist are progressively extended and applied to new fields, the scope of pure philosophical speculation is progressively narrowed. In the seventeenth century the scientist and the philosopher were not definitely and clearly distinguished as they are to-day; what we call physical science was by Newton and his predecessors called 'natural philosophy'. Most of the great philosophers of the century – Descartes, Spinoza and Leibniz – were philosopher-mathematicians or philosopher-scientists; philosophical speculation and experimental science were not yet disentangled. In what A. N. Whitehead described as 'the century of genius', modern experimental science was in its infancy, and it was largely by the philosophers, or rather the philosopher-mathematicians, that it was taught to speak. Their speculations about Matter, Motion, Space, Energy, Ultimate Particles, and Infinitesimal Magnitudes supplied the ideas with the aid of which modern physics was gradually built; these very abstract speculations about the Universe, which we are now apt to reject as unscientific and worthless because they were not properly based on experiment, did in fact supply the indispensable background for experiment; for (to adapt a phrase from Kant) if ideas without experiment are empty, so experiment without ideas is blind; experimental science must generally arise out of speculation, because experiment does not generally lead to a body of organized knowledge unless the experimenter has been supplied with some framework of ideas into which his results are to be fitted, and which will guide him in his experiments; he generally starts with some suggested programme which prescribes the terms to be used in describing what he observes. Certainly the framework of ideas used in the early (or even in the later) phases of any modern science is not rigid, but is adapted and radically altered as experiment proceeds; some or all of the old concepts of Matter or Space or Energy, which emerged from early speculation by philosopher-scientists, are subsequently discarded as no longer useful, and the work of speculation or concept-forming is largely left to experimental scientists to perform in the light of their own discoveries. As knowledge based on experiment grows, there is no further need or even possibility of purely abstract speculation; so the philosopher-scientist or metaphysician, with his system of ideas designed to explain the workings of the Universe, is gradually superseded by an army of experimenters, each working in a specialized field on specific and defined problems.

Spinoza was a speculative metaphysician in the heroic age of modern speculation, the age in which the foundations of modern physical knowledge were being laid. In histories of modern philosophy he is generally classified with Descartes and Leibniz as a 'rationalist'; at least one justification of the use of this label is that each of these three philosophers sought in their systems to prescribe how the world could be made intelligible to human reason; each of them in effect provided a model or programme of a possible perfect scientific knowledge of the order of Nature. Their ideals and programmes of natural knowledge were widely different, and they set different limits to the possible range of human knowledge, and of the understanding of Nature. But they agreed in the reasoned optimism with which they laid down the outlines of a rational method by the use of which the world might be made intelligible; their greatness was in the exaltation of the powers of reason and of rational methods at the expense of blind faith, supernatural revelation and theological mystery.

Their pattern of rational method, of clear and consecutive thinking by means of which the truth in any inquiry could infallibly be obtained and recognized, was mathematics; for only in mathematics is pure reason recognized as the sole arbiter, and allowed to operate by itself and without restrictions; it seemed that the mathematician's proofs are so designed that they cannot be doubted or disputed; it seemed that within mathematics error can infallibly be detected, and that there is no possibility of the conflicting opinions and undecidable disputes which are typical of traditional philosophy and of all other forms of human knowledge. When Descartes, an original mathematician himself, writes of the ideal form of knowledge and method of inquiry as involving only 'clear and distinct ideas', his example of the reasoning which involves only clear and distinct ideas is mathematical reasoning; similarly when Spinoza gives an example to illustrate what he means by genuine knowledge, the example is a proposition of mathematics. The programme of the rationalist philosophers in the seventeenth century, that is, of those philosophers who tried to prescribe how the human intellect could achieve clear and certain knowledge of the world, was to generalize the mathematical method of reasoning, and to apply it without restriction to all the problems of philosophy and science. The arguments of Euclid lead to conclusions which are for ever certain and indubitable; their truth is evident in the 'natural light' of reason; if we apply this mathematical method of starting from clear and distinctly defined ideas, and of advancing from them by a succession of logical steps each of which involves only clear and distinct ideas, we cannot go wrong, whatever be the subject-matter of our inquiry; since the premise and every subsequent step in the argument will commend itself to the natural light of reason as self-evident, the conclusion must be finally accepted as self-evident and as undeniably true by all men capable of thinking clearly and distinctly. Outside mathematics, and most conspicuously in attempts to answer philosophical problems about Mind and Matter and God, argument had for centuries been confused and inconclusive, only because philosophers had failed to purge their minds of all ideas which are not clear and distinct; they had failed to follow the mathematicians' example in taking as their starting-point propositions which are immediately self-evident, and which consist solely of ideas which are clearly and distinctly conceived. For centuries the schoolmen had floundered among apparently undecidable disputes, because they had not clarified their ideas or defined their terms in the sense in which the mathematician clarifies his ideas and defines his terms. They had been hopelessly confused, because, unlike mathematicians, they did not rely in their arguments solely on the natural light of pure reason, but in part at least on imagination; and imagination, according to both Descartes and Spinoza, is the prime source of confusion of thought and so the prime source of error.

The distinction between pure reason and imagination is essential to the understanding of the intellectual background of Spinoza's education and thought, as it is to the understanding of any part of European literature and thought in the seventeenth century; and it has its effective origin in Descartes' method of clear and distinct ideas. When we attend to and are convinced by a proof in Euclid, our assent to its conclusion is independent of the particular images of straight lines or triangles which may occur to us while we read the proof or rehearse it to ourselves. The self-evident truth of the conclusion depends solely on those conceptions (not the images) of a straight line and a triangle which are involved; as soon as we have understood what is meant by these terms, that is, as soon as we have formed a clear and distinct idea of a triangle and a straight line, we accept the conclusion as true, whatever images or mental pictures (and these be many of many different kinds) may happen to be associated with the proposition. The terms of a proposition are clearly conceived or understood in so far as the words which occur in its expression do not derive their meaning from any particular images which may from time to time be associated with them; for instance, I can be said to have in this sense a clear idea of God in so far as the word 'God' is not indissolubly connected in my mind with any particular image or images (e.g. of an old man above the clouds), but stands for a notion or concept which is logically connected with other ideas (e.g. of omnipotence and omniscience), exactly as the concept of a three-angled figure is logically connected with the idea of a three-sided figure. Most men, even those who, as philosophers, are supposed to be capable of thought which is in this sense abstract, in fact lapse when thinking and arguing into a figurative or imaginative use of language; when thinking of the attributes of God, they come to accept some propositions as true, which, when examined, are seen to depend, not on any clearly defined conception of divinity, but on some particular imaginative picture which they have formed of God. Words or symbols within mathematics do not derive their meaning from the figures or images which may be used to illustrate them, but stand for clearly defined conceptions. If a similar clarity, rigour and certainty are ever to be achieved in philosophy and natural knowledge, their terms must first be purged of all the figurative and subjective associations of ordinary discourse; their vocabulary must be formed of words which are logical counters having a purely intellectual significance, words which stand in this sense for clear and distinct ideas. This conception of pure reasoning or Intellect is common to Descartes, Spinoza and Leibniz and gives the second important sense of the label 'rationalist'; it is necessarily connected with a doctrine of language and style which, directly or indirectly, influenced the whole of European literature, until the Romantic Movement towards the end of the eighteenth century made Imagination mean something more than the vice of unclarity and unreason. In the Cartesian and classical age the language of rational discourse had to be as far as possible free from figurative or metaphorical expressions; or at least the figurative or imaginative use of expressions must be recognized as purely decorative; such a style was in fact characteristic of the great French classical writers of the seventeenth century and of most of their successors both within and outside France before the Revolution. Philosophy in the age of Descartes, Spinoza, and Leibniz was in part written in a learned Latin which, having largely lost its poetical and conversational uses, could be made entirely formal and abstract and, therefore, in Descartes' sense, extremely clear; words could be given a precise technical meaning, comparatively unconnected with any of their shifting and figurative uses in ordinary speech. Descartes further wrote French prose which has always been a model of absolute clarity and simplicity and he exhibited an ease in handling abstractions which has never been achieved in any other modern European language. Leibniz, having himself written in the bare Latin and French which was the common currency of the learned world, actually proposed the creation of an artificial symbolic language in which every clear and simple idea would have a single symbol; so, all the symbols being governed by rules prescribing their possible combinations, all abstract reasoning would be reduced to mere algebraical calculations. This project of what Leibniz called a *Characteristica Universalis* was the extreme and logical development of the common rationalist doctrine that error and uncertainty are due to the unclarity of ordinary spoken and literary languages, which are not designed to convey clear and distinct ideas.

Great divergences between Descartes' and Spinoza's thought and purpose will emerge at every stage in this exposition; to treat Spinoza primarily as a follower and disciple of Descartes, as he has often been treated, is, I believe, largely to misconstrue and misrepresent him. But a particular philosophy may permeate the thought of an age so thoroughly that even those who explicitly revolt against its declared doctrines are subsequently seen to have accepted, consciously or unconsciously, its underlying assumptions and methods; even those who to-day, for example, most explicitly repudiate Marx's theory of politics and history have absorbed many of his ideas, which have passed into common currency. Cartesianism – construed not as a set of particular doctrines or propositions, but as a whole vocabulary and a method of argument – dominated philosophical and scientific thought in seventeenth-century Europe (though less in England than elsewhere), as Aristotelianism, similarly construed, had dominated Europe in previous centuries. Spinoza had steeped himself in Descartes' philosophy, and his first written work was a methodical exposition of it (*Metaphysical Thoughts*). But at a very early stage, and even before he wrote his exposition of it, he had rejected its conclusions and had proceeded in his own thought far beyond it, having discovered in Descartes what seemed to him radical incoherences; he saw, or thought he saw, demonstrable contradictions in Descartes' conceptions of Substance, of the relation of Thought and Extension, of the relation between God and the created universe, of Free-will and Necessity, of Error, and lastly, of the distinction between Intellect and the Imagination. Descartes seemed to have stopped short in developing his own doctrines to their extreme logical conclusions, partly perhaps because he foresaw some at least of the uncomfortable moral and theological consequences which must ensue; he was a rationalist who not only remained undisturbed within the Catholic Church, but even provided the Church with new armour to protect its essential doctrines against the dangerous implications of the new mathematical physics and the new method in philosophy. Descartes was not rigidly consistent in maintaining the distinction between Intellect and the Imagination, and even speaks of Imagination as essential to mathematical reasoning, though it is the source of confusion in metaphysics; yet he urges the application of mathematical reasoning to metaphysics. Perhaps his crucial hesitation is whether our idea of God can be purely intellectual or must be in part imaginative – that is, whether God's nature can be in any sense understood unless we can describe his attributes in terms which derive their meaning from ordinary experience. If the use of ordinary terms is essential to understanding, our conception of God must be, in part at least, an anthropomorphic one; but if all images and so all anthropomorphism are removed, the word 'God' loses many of its traditional Christian connotations, and the believer is left, as Spinoza showed, with an utterly abstract and impersonal Deity. Spinoza made the distinction between Intellect and Imagination, between pure logical thinking and the confused association of ideas, one of the foundations of his system; unlike Descartes, he throughout applied the distinction rigorously and accepted every consequence of it. At every stage in the *Ethics*, and in reply to objections in his correspondence, he insists that his words, and particularly his words about God and his attributes, must never be understood in their vulgar and figurative sense, but only in the special sense given to them in his definitions. He considered almost everything which had been written and said about God, and about his creation of the Universe, as meaningless, unphilosophical men being incapable of conceiving God clearly; for they are by training incapable of understanding what they cannot imagine. Any image or mental picture must be a projection of our own sense-experience; we can only form a picture from elements of our experience. But God, essentially and by his nature, is wholly outside our experience, and cannot be properly described by imaginative analogy with anything within our experience; he must be conceived by an effort of pure thought. Similarly, all the other terms which we use in our philosophical thinking, that is, in our attempt to understand the Universe as a whole, must be carefully examined to ensure that they really do represent to us clearly-defined intellectual conceptions, as opposed to confused images or pictures derived from our sense-experience.

If therefore Descartes was a rationalist, in the sense that he advocated the solution of all problems of natural knowledge by the application of the mathematical method of pure reasoning, Spinoza was doubly a rationalist in this sense; in fact no other philosopher has ever insisted more uncompromisingly that all problems, whether metaphysical, moral or scientific, must be formulated and solved as purely intellectual problems, as if they were theorems in geometry. Principally for this reason he wrote both his early exposition of Descartes' philosophy and his own great definitive work, the *Ethics*, in the geometrical manner, as a succession of propositions with supporting proofs, lemmas and corollaries. He thus eliminated from the presentation of his philosophy the concealed means of persuasion and of engaging the imagination of the reader which are part of ordinary prose-writing; he wished the true philosophy to be presented in a form which was, as nearly as possible, as objective and as free from appeals to the imagination as is Euclid's *Elements*. He wished to be entirely effaced as individual and author, being no more than the mouthpiece of pure Reason. In the already quoted autobiographical passage from *On the Correction of the Understanding*, designed as a relatively popular work, he follows Descartes in stating the purpose of his philosophy in terms of the occasion which prompted him to begin his inquiry. Thereafter his own personality is never allowed to appear through the text; in the *Ethics* it does not reveal itself even in the most indirect ways, not even in the selection of illustrations or in idiosyncrasies of style. This majestic impersonality is even more conspicuous in what survives of his philosophical correspondence; even in his letters, some of them addressed to personal friends, the philosophical argument is deployed straitly and rigorously, and only occasionally, when intolerably provoked by the obscurantism of some moralizing or devout critic, does he allow a note of irony or of indignation to appear.

But this very impersonality becomes a distinguishing personal style; Spinoza's writing, whether on personal, moral, political or the most remote metaphysical issues, can always be recognized by a certain grave remorseless-ness of logic, a complete absence of decoration, and a

sustained concentration which admits of no concession to
the desire to please; and such a style, which, owing to its
lack of literary artifice and high degree of abstraction,
survives even in translation, has a peculiar fascination, as
soon as its purposes are understood and respected. His
philosophy is an experiment in impassive rationalism
carried to its extreme limits; we are required to think about
God and our own desires and passions with exactly the
same detachment and clarity as in the study of geometry
we think about triangles and circles. In the capacity so to
think lies our supreme and only happiness and freedom,
and only in so far as we exercise it do we become anything
more than insignificant fragments of the infinite, self-
creating Universe.

To introduce Spinoza's philosophy under any particular
label, as primarily a development of Cartesianism or of
any other previous pattern of thought, is demonstrably
wrong, if only as a matter of history. That he escapes all
ready-made labels or classifications emerges most clearly
in the variety of points of view from which he has been
both attacked and defended. Within his own lifetime he
was regarded as the destroyer of all established religion and
morality; the *Ethics* itself could not safely be published
while he was alive, and Leibniz, perhaps the only contemporary who could fully appreciate his greatness as a philosopher, dared not acknowledge any sympathy with his ideas.
For about a hundred years after his death and the posthumous publication of the *Ethics*, his name occurs rarely in
philosophical or other literature and is generally linked with

some standardized phrase of abuse, pointing to the dangerous immorality of his doctrines. There is little evidence that his work was seriously studied or understood before Lessing and Goethe first awakened interest in him. Hume and Voltaire made slighting references to his shocking doctrines, but it is unlikely that either of them (certainly not Voltaire) seriously studied the *Ethics*; he was condemned in Bayle's *Dictionary*, which was then the source-book for philosophy used by all rational and free-thinking men. Spinoza's philosophy evoked no sympathetic echo in the eighteenth century, since his grand *a priori* method of argument repelled the sceptical, as his subversion of Christian theology repelled the devout. Like the great Italian philosopher, Vico, and a very few other figures in the history of thought, he was born precociously, a hundred years before a climate of thought existed in which his greatness could be recognized. But from Goethe's admiration of him until the present time, Spinoza's philosophy has had a curious double history which is a true reflexion of his originality; for to some he has appeared primarily as a man obsessed with God, a pantheist who interprets every natural phenomenon as a revelation of an immanent but impersonal God; to others he has appeared as a harsh materialist and determinist who denies all significance to morality and religion. His philosophy, with its genuine double-aspect, has been an inspiration to two types of mind, and has been interpreted in two traditions. He has been admired, for instance, by Marxists as supposedly a materialist and certainly a determinist; yet his foremost English expositor, the late H. H. Joachim, saw in Spinoza anticipations of his own Idealist philosophy. To George Eliot, who began a translation of his works, he was the enemy of superstition and the hero of scientific rationalism and materialism; to Coleridge and Shelley he communicated an almost mystical sense of the ideal unity of Nature. But throughout the nineteenth century he appeared as the philosopher who had exalted and displayed the powers of objective and dispassionate reason beyond all other philosophers, and for this reason was admired by such men as Renan, Flaubert, Matthew Arnold, and Anatole France.

As in his effects, so in his sources and the influences which formed his thought, Spinoza is a peculiar and isolated figure, in part standing aside from the main currents of European philosophy. His early education was largely in the strait and enclosed tradition of orthodox Jewry. He was a scholar trained in one of the most severe of all intellectual disciplines. He broke its bounds and revolted against it, as he must have revolted against all orthodoxies. But he carried with him, not only suggestions from the theology and Biblical criticism of Maimonides (1135–1204) and from a great line of Jewish scholars and theologians, but also the prophetic conception of philosophy as a search for salvation. Although salvation by reason is substituted in his philosophy for salvation by revelation and obedience, his moral severity, particularly if compared with the worldly urbanity of Descartes, is often reminiscent of the Old Testament, even in the tone and accent of his writing. It has been remarked (by Sir F. Pollock) that, even though the *Ethics* contains a thorough survey of the powers and passions of men, Spinoza only once casually mentions any form of art, and he seems to have attached no importance to aesthetic experience in his scheme of human development and happiness; and this is only one symptom of his general detachment from Greek and Mediterranean influences.

As a Jew severed from his community, equally at ease in several languages, absorbed in no national community, he was free, unattached and alone; and in this freedom and solitude, which he deliberately reinforced and protected, he set himself to construct by pure reason, and without appeal to any authority, a philosophy which he believed would be demonstrably complete and final.

CHAPTER TWO
Outline of Metaphysics

THE *Ethics* is divided into five parts, of which the first is entitled *Concerning God*. The Definitions, Axioms and Propositions with which the book begins must not be regarded, in spite of the geometrical arrangement, solely as the ultimate premises from which the later propositions are deduced; and no one should allow himself to be discouraged from reading further because he cannot understand or accept the very first definitions and propositions of this first part. These first definitions and propositions can be properly understood only in the light of the propositions which follow them in the order of exposition; they form a system of mutually supporting propositions, and as soon as one has understood any one of them, one ought in theory to be able to derive and explain any of the others as its necessary consequence. In the first part of the *Ethics* Spinoza is in effect introducing a set of definitions and elucidations of each of his fundamental notions of Substance, Cause, Attribute, Freedom, and Necessity, successively explaining each in terms of the others; with the aid of these logically connected notions he defines what he means by God or Nature. But although the order in which these definitions are presented may be in part arbitrary, in Spinoza's view the definitions themselves are certainly not arbitrary; they are not offered as one of a set of alternative possible and convenient definitions of Substance, Cause and God, but as the only possible or consistent set of definitions; to conceive the world except in terms of these notions, so defined, is demonstrably to be involved in contradiction or to be using words without attaching any clear meaning to them. And it is to this demonstration of inter-connectedness that one must attend in order to understand the force of the argument.

It is natural to begin with the notion of substance, a notion which has a continuous history in philosophy from Aristotle to Descartes. Philosophers had developed the distinction between a substance and its attributes partly in order to mark the logical difference between the ultimate subjects of knowledge or judgement and what we can know or say about these subjects, and partly also to answer puzzles about change and identity; the subject of a judgement, that which we know about, may significantly be said to possess different qualities at different times, while itself persisting through time as an identifiable subject with a whole series of different qualities inhering in it. Whenever we make a statement and add to our knowledge, we are saying of some subject or substance that it possesses some quality or attribute, or perhaps that it stands in some relation to some other subject or substance. The next step is to divide the attributes of a substance – or the qualities which it may be said to possess – into two categories: first, the essential or defining attributes or properties, those which make it the kind of thing it is, and, secondly, the accidental attributes, which it may acquire and lose without changing its essential nature; in Spinoza's terminology the words 'necessary' and 'contingent' are generally substituted for 'essential' and 'accidental'. The traditional doctrine was that we know the essence or real nature of a substance when we know what are its essential attributes; the essential attributes are the defining attributes of the substance, and to state what attributes are included in the essence of a substance is to state what makes the substance what it is. Such 'real' definitions are not intended to be mere conventions about the use of words, but are to be taken as explanations of the essential nature of whatever is the object of study; they are the discoveries in which any rational inquiry culminates, and, within this classic theory of knowledge or science, a real definition can be said to be the proper expression of genuine knowledge. We arrive at these real definitions by a process of thought often described as intuitive induction; we observe the concomitance of a group of attributes inhering in a substance, and as a result of this observation we come to see a logically necessary connexion between the attributes; we grasp or apprehend intuitively that it is of the essence of being a man that any man must be rational, and we grasp immediately that all men as such must possess this characteristic. The concept of substance, which is central in Spinoza's metaphysics, is attached historically to this conception of scientific knowledge as the discovery of the essential nature or the real definitions of the various natural kinds of entity existing in the Universe; this is the conception of scientific knowledge which is contained in the traditional Aristotelian logic. Aristotelian logic provided a pattern and programme of scientific inquiry as consisting essentially of *classification* of things into definable natural kinds, the kinds of things to be found in the Universe being discriminated by their different essential qualities or attributes. Before experimental science could begin, it seemed first necessary to compile a systematic inventory or catalogue of the various kinds of things to be studied. Within such a logic of classification – and many sciences began with classification or inventory-making and so needed such a logic – the standard or model form of proposition was taken to be the subject-predicate form, that is, the form of statement which says that a thing or substance possesses a certain quality or attribute; scientific knowledge at this early stage of its development was conceived as the cataloguing of the essential qualitative differences to be found in Nature. With the growth of mathematical physics from Galileo onwards, involving the search for general quantitative laws in Nature, the conception of scientific knowledge as consisting essentially of qualitative classification was gradually undermined; naturally therefore the logical terminology associated with the predominantly classificatory phases of science was re-examined and was increasingly called in question by philosopher-scientists as inadequate for their purposes. Among the notions called for re-examination in seventeenth-century philosophy was the conception of the world as a plurality of substances, each persisting through time in possession of certain essential attributes; the possibility of a plurality of substances had been denied many times from the beginnings of philosophy, but was to be denied again by Spinoza for largely new reasons and with a new force and emphasis.

One of the most evident difficulties of applying the notion of substance is that, if the universe is conceived to consist of a plurality of substances, that is, of ultimate subjects each of which can be said to possess certain essential attributes, these substances must be conceived to interact; it seems that changes of state occurring in the history of one substance must produce changes of state in the history of another. If such causal interaction among substances is not admitted, then any natural event must be conceived to be adequately describable as a change of quality occurring in the history of any one of a number of substances, each of which is causally unrelated to any other; the natural order is then represented as consisting of a multitude of substances, all of whose states can be explained in terms of their own essential natures, and not in terms of the action of any other substance upon them; and roughly this conception of Nature as a system of self-determining substances, called monads, was reached by Leibniz, Spinoza's contemporary; his philosophy was the result of working out to its logical conclusion the notion of a plurality of substances each possessing an essential nature of its own. But if the substances do interact, then the succession of their states cannot be wholly explained in terms of their own essential natures; for some of their

states, or modifications of their nature, will be the effect of
the action of external substances upon them.

This problem of how substances can be said to interact introduces the notion of cause; substances are
essentially things which originate change in accordance
with the laws of their own nature; the notion of cause
therefore occurs, inseparably connected with that of
substance and attribute, in the first few propositions of the
Ethics. The word 'cause', as it is generally used in rationalist philosophies and throughout Spinoza's writing, must
be divested of many of its present associations, and
particularly of its association with the causal laws of
modern experimental science. What is common to
Spinoza's use and to our contemporary use of the word is
simply that a cause is taken to be anything which *explains*
the existence or qualities of the effect; but the two senses of
explanation are widely different, following the differences
in the pattern of scientific knowledge envisaged. To
Spinoza (and by definition to all rationalist philosophers)
to 'explain' means to show that one true proposition is the
logically necessary consequence of some other; explanation
essentially involves exhibiting necessary connexions, and
'necessary connexion' in this context means a strictly
logical connexion to be discovered by logical analysis of
the ideas involved. The ideal of scientific explanation is
here purely deductive and mathematical; Euclid's geometry provides the standard example of genuine explanation, in that Euclid is concerned only with the purely
logical dependence of the possession of one property or

properties on the possession of others. Thus, to understand why a substance possesses the attributes which it does, and to explain the modifications, or changes of state, which it undergoes, is to exhibit these attributes or modifications as the logical consequence of other attributes or modifications. If substances causally interact, in the sense that changes of state or modifications of one may be the causes of modifications of the other, then the modifications of any one of these interacting substances cannot be explained solely as the effects of its own essential nature; this leads to a fundamental distinction; those of a substance's attributes or modifications which are not to be explained as the necessary consequences of its own essential nature can be distinguished as accidental (as opposed to essential) or contingent (as opposed to necessary). A substance, all of whose attributes and modifications can be deduced from its own essential nature, and all of whose attributes are therefore necessary and not contingent, can be described as 'cause of itself' (*causa sui*); and only such a substance can be so described. It is Spinoza's fundamental argument in Part I of the *Ethics* that there *can* be only *one* substance which is *causa sui*, and that this single substance must be identified with the universe conceived as a whole; this unique all-inclusive totality he therefore calls 'God or Nature' (*Deus sive Natura*). The force of his argument, depending on the strict use of the notions of cause and substance in the traditional sense, is that any other assumption or interpretation must infallibly lead to contradiction.

The argument, with its conclusion that the notion of a plurality of substances involves a contradiction, clearly must depend on some restriction in the definition of substance, and this restriction must be such as to exclude the possibility of distinguishing between the essential or necessary and the accidental or contingent attributes of a substance; for we have seen that the simple traditional notion of a plurality of substances logically involved the maintenance of this distinction between essential and accidental properties. Spinoza's definition of substance in the *Ethics* (*Pt.* I. *Def.* III) does in fact impose just such a restriction: 'I understand substance to be that which is in itself and is conceived through itself: I mean that, the conception of which can be formed independently of the conception of another thing.' The full meaning of this definition emerges in *Propositions* II, III, and VI, which depend upon it: 'Two substances, which have different attributes, have nothing in common between them' (*Ethics Pt.* I. *Prop.* II): 'Of two things having nothing in common between them, one cannot be the cause of the other' (*Ethics Pt.* I. *Prop.* III). 'One substance cannot be produced by another' (*Ethics Pt.* I. *Prop.* VI); 'for', as Spinoza writes in supporting *Prop.* VI, 'if a substance can be produced from anything else, knowledge of it would depend upon knowledge of its cause (*Axiom* IV), and consequently (*Def.* III) it would not be a substance.' In other words, he has so strictly defined substance that nothing whose attributes are the effects of outside causes can be called a substance; a substance by definition is such that all its attributes or modifications can be explained in terms of its own nature.

If the Universe were conceived to consist of two (or more) such substances – and Descartes, in his all-embracing distinction between Thought and Extension, the mental and the physical worlds, had in effect made this supposition – then an explanation would be required of why just two (or more) such substances exist; for, according to Spinoza (*Ethics Pt.* I. *Axioms* III and IV), everything can be explained as the effect of some cause, and to suppose anything else is immediately to abandon the hope of rational understanding; for rational understanding simply consists in knowledge of causes. But, if more than one substance is admitted, to provide an explanation of their nature must be to represent these two (or more) substances as the effects of causes other than themselves; but this is contrary to their definition, as being causes of themselves; therefore the assumption of more than one such substance leads to contradiction and is impossible. There can be only one substance so defined, and nothing can exist independently of, or distinct from, this single substance; everything which exists must be conceived as an attribute or modification of, or as in some way inherent in, this single substance; this substance is therefore to be identified with Nature conceived as an intelligible whole. This substance must be infinite in its nature, because, if it were finite, there could be supposed something outside or other than it, which limits it or constitutes its boundary; but then it could not be single or unique, which it has been proved to be; and therefore the single substance, which is Nature conceived as a whole, must be essentially infinite; and this involves saying that it possesses an infinite number of attributes each of which is itself infinite. In Spinoza's inherited use of the word, 'infinite' can be applied to whatever is necessarily and by definition unlimited or unbounded; to say of something that it is infinite is to say that nothing can exist distinguishable from it which can affect or modify it; it is the necessary and defining characteristic of anything which is finite to be limited and to be liable to be affected or modified by things other than itself.

God is by definition (*Ethics Pt.* I. *Def.* VI) – and this definition is in accordance with orthodox theological and scholastic uses of the word 'God' – the being who possesses infinite attributes; therefore the single substance, which is identified with Nature conceived as a whole, is also properly identified with God. Thus Spinoza's logic leads remorselessly to the phrase, which shocked the pious, *Deus sive Natura*, as the inevitable name [1] of the unique, infinite and all-inclusive Substance. It is on account of this phrase that Spinoza has been alternately abhorred and venerated as a pantheist, 'pantheism' meaning the identification of God with Nature. Pantheism is usually a doctrine associated with mystical intuitions or with a poetical and

---

[1] Perhaps *Deus sive Natura* is intended to be a proper name in a peculiar and technical sense of 'proper name' which interests logicians; it is introduced as *necessarily* having *unique* reference: it is unlike other names in that there is only one thing to which it can be applied.

romantic feeling of the splendour and unity of Nature. But Spinoza's identification of God with Nature, however indirectly inspiring it may later have been to the poets of the Romantic Movement, in intention at least owes nothing to poetical imagination; it is conceived to be the outcome of exact definition and rigorous logic. When attacked or asked to elucidate further, he returns repeatedly in his *Letters*, as also in the explanatory passages of the *Ethics*, to what seems to him the clear logical necessity of this identification; it is the interference of the imagination, leading us to associate the word 'God' with anthropomorphic and personal images, which obstructs our reason in the recognition of the logical necessity of the identification. As soon as we dissociate the word 'God' from all figurative descriptions and images and no longer try to picture the deity as a person, mere logic must lead us to recognize that God and Nature cannot possibly be distinguished.

The vulgar distinction, based on imagination and not on reason, between God and Nature has always been tied to the distinction between the Creator and his Creation; God is imagined as an artificer and Nature, including man, as his artifact. As God is generally imagined as a super-person, a will and purpose, in the same sense in which these words are applied to men, are attributed to him also. By trying to imagine God the Creator in accordance with this human analogy, theologians and metaphysicians have involved themselves in perennial contradictions and controversies – e.g. over the problem of evil, of God's freedom of choice and his reasons for choosing the actual world in preference to other possible worlds. To Spinoza this popular and traditional Christian idea of God the Creator seems a fiction of the imagination; when analysed logically, it can be demonstrated to involve a contradiction in terms. It can be proved that there can only be one self-dependent substance in the strict sense, that is, one ultimate subject all of whose attributes or modifications are explicable in terms of its own nature; this substance must be essentially infinite, that is, possess an infinity of infinite attributes, and must be identified with Nature conceived as a whole; for if it were not identified with Nature as a whole, there would exist something other than the Substance itself, and no cause could be found of the existence of this other thing, unless it were a Substance, 'cause of itself': but a plurality of substances is impossible. The unique, self-determining and all-inclusive substance cannot, by definition, be created or produced by anything other than itself; therefore the notion of a Creator distinct from his creation contains an evident contradiction, involving, as it must, the conception of two substances, one the cause of the other. The common Jewish and Christian idea of creation necessarily involves this dualism, which Spinoza's definition of substance excludes as self-contradictory. But, what is more important, if the definition, from which the necessity of monism follows, is challenged, a Spinozist can point in justification of this definition to the antinomies which the distinction between the Creator and his Creation necessarily involves. One destructive argument (there are several) proceeds as follows: If God is distinguished from Nature, which he creates, then God cannot be infinite and all-powerful, because there exists something other than, or distinguishable from, God, which limits God's power and perfection; on this assumption God cannot be either infinite or perfect, because *ex hypothesi* Nature, being distinguished from God, must possess some attributes which God does not possess (*Ethics Pt.* I. *Prop.* IV). But a God who is finite and imperfect is a contradiction in terms. Similar reductions to absurdity can be constructed in terms of the notions of necessity and contingency and also of cause and effect.

Spinoza expresses his rejection of the commonplace distinction between the Creator and his creation by the use of a traditional theological distinction; *Proposition* XVIII (*Ethics Pt.* I) states that God is the immanent and enduring, and not the transient, cause of all things. If God is conceived as the agent who set the Universe in motion by a single act, or set of acts, of creation, then he is properly described as its transient cause; on this (according to Spinoza, self-contradictory) assumption, God's causal activity occurred at some particular time and then ceased, as do human activities, and is therefore not eternal. On this interpretation we do not need to refer to God in our explanations of change in the Universe, except when we trace the changes back to their First Cause. It was this conception of God as transient cause, the prime mover who set the Universe in motion in accordance with fixed laws of motion, which on the whole commended itself to uncritical scientific common sense, both before and after Newton; it was convenient in scientific practice to regard the Universe as a giant clock-work mechanism, which, once wound up and set in motion by the Supreme Clock-maker in accordance with his design and laws of motion, revolved on its own (except perhaps for occasional inter-ferences in the mechanism by the maker, called miracles). The advantage of this conception, as developed in the great Deist compromise of the eighteenth century, was that it allowed men of science and men of religion to declare their doctrines and discoveries without the danger of mutual trespass or conflict. The scientist could investigate the laws of nature, while acknowledging that the laws which he discovered were evidence of God's design; the theologian, while accepting the existence of natural laws as evidence of God's purposeful design, could speak of the act of creation as a mystery and as the test of faith.

But Spinoza's conception of God as immanent cause involves regarding God as the eternal cause of all things, where 'eternal' is opposed to 'occurring and then ceasing'; no date can significantly be attached to God's causal efficacy or to his act of creation; for this would involve representing the Creation as an event, or series of events, *within* the temporal order of natural events, a conception which must lead (and has in fact led theologians) into perplexities. In the name of common sense, which is so often a synonym for the confused ideas of the imagination, critics of Spinoza, some contemporaries and many later, have misunderstood what he meant by God as immanent cause; if isolated from its context within his philosophy, the notion seems merely mystical and anti-scientific, seeming to imply that natural things or events must be explained as the effects of supernatural and not of natural causes. In fact the implication is exactly the reverse; it is rather that natural things or events cannot be explained by transcendent causes or by a transcendent cause. The doctrine appears mystical or unscientific in its tendency only if one forgets that in Spinoza's use the word 'God' is interchangeable with the word 'Nature'. To say that God is the immanent cause of all things is another way of saying that everything must be explained as belonging to the single and all-inclusive system which is Nature, and no cause (not even a First Cause) can be conceived as somehow outside or independent of the order of Nature. Any doctrine of a transcendent God, since 'transcendent' simply means 'outside the order of Nature', or any doctrine of God as Creator distinguished as transient cause from his creation, involves this impossibility; for it introduces the mystery of an inexplicable act of creation, an act which is somehow outside the order of events in Nature. God, or Nature, as the eternal cause of all things and of itself, must be conceived to be free in its self-creative activity; for 'that thing is said to be free which exists by mere necessity of its own nature and is determined in its actions by itself alone' (*Ethics Pt.* I. *Def.* VII); this definition applies to God or Nature as a whole, and can apply to nothing else. Of anything less than the unique self-creating substance which is the whole of Nature, one cannot say that its existence and attributes can be explained without reference to anything other than itself. Only God or Nature as a whole is self-creating; it follows, therefore, that only God or Nature is absolutely free. From this argument we derive quite simply what is the most far-reaching proposition of Spinoza's philosophy. 'In the nature of things nothing contingent is admitted, but all things are determined by the necessity of divine nature to exist and act in a certain way' (*Ethics Pt.* I. *Prop.* XXIX). *Within* Nature everything must be determined, at least in the sense in which 'determined' implies 'not self-caused or self-creating'; everything which is within Nature, if intelligible at all, must be in this sense determined, since its existence must be deducible, directly or indirectly, within the system of the unique substance which is God or Nature; and it has been shown to be meaningless to imagine anything outside Nature, in Spinoza's sense of this word; therefore it follows that everything in the Universe is determined and nothing is contingent. Within Spinoza's logic and presuppositions this momentous conclusion cannot be avoided, however often one looks around in search of an escape; and it always seemed to him, like the other fundamental propositions of his system, so self-evident and irresistible, that he could only attribute (in the notes in the *Ethics* and in his letters) the resistance which it provoked to a refusal to think clearly and to attend to necessary definitions. If the Universe is intelligible, everything within it must be conceived to be determined by necessary causes; this implication seemed to him as intrinsically self-evident as one of the more simple theorems in Euclid; it can only be because our sentiments and passions are engaged, and because popular speech reflects our actual ignorance of the laws of Nature, that we feel such a strong resistance to it.

God or Nature is a free and originating cause, and the only free, because the only self-creating, cause; in so far as we think, as we always can, of God or Nature as the free and self-creating cause, we think of Nature, in Spinoza's phrase, as *Natura Naturans*, Nature actively creating herself and deploying her essential powers in her infinite attributes and in the various modes of these attributes. But we can also think of Nature (and this is the more general connotation of the word outside Spinoza's philosophy) as the system of what is created. Nature is conceived in its passive capacity, as an established system, or as *Natura Naturata*, in Spinoza's phrase. Throughout Spinoza's philosophy use is made of this difficult device of conceiving what is in essence or reality the same thing, as manifesting itself in two different ways, or as having two different aspects (a vague word which one is sometimes driven to use in this context). It is equally correct to think of God or Nature as the unique creator (*Natura Naturans*) and as the unique creation (*Natura Naturata*); it is not only correct, but necessary to attach both of these complementary meanings to the word, neither being complete, or even possible, as a conception of Nature without the other. This doctrine of the essential identity of the Creator and his Creation, so far from being mystical and anti-scientific in intention, leads logically to the conclusion that every single thing in the Universe necessarily belongs to, or falls within, a single intelligible, causal system. To have complete knowledge of the cause of the existence or activity of anything must ultimately involve having complete knowledge of the whole order of Nature; if we are to provide a complete explanation of the existence and activity of anything in the Universe, we must be able to deduce the existence and activity of the thing studied from the essential attributes and modes of the self-creating God or Nature. This so-called pantheistic doctrine can in fact be fairly represented as the metaphysical expression of the ideal or programme of a unified science, that is, of a completed science which would enable every natural change to be shown as a completely determined effect within a single system of causes; everything must be explicable within a single theory. This ideal or programme has always fascinated theoreticians of science, and has been re-stated as a logical, and not metaphysical, thesis within the present century; a programme which could be intelligently expressed in the seventeenth century in metaphysical terms, as an *a priori* thesis about the creation and structure of the Universe, can intelligibly be expressed in this century in logical terms, as an *a priori* thesis about the structure of the language of science. Such interpretations of metaphysical theories in terms of modern logic are legitimate and even necessary, provided that it is always remembered that they are interpretations and not expositions; it may be illuminating and even necessary to translate philosophical doctrines into modern terminologies unknown to their authors; it can only be misleading if one represents the result of the translation as the explicit intention of the authors. Spinoza did not envisage a unified science, in the modern sense of these words, if only because he did not mean by 'cause' and 'knowledge' what we mean in this context. But his conception of the unity of Nature, within which everything can in principle be made intelligible to reason as the effect of some cause, is, on any interpretation, a thesis of scientific optimism and an invitation to rational inquiry, and not an appeal to mystical intuition.

To summarize: God or Nature is eternal, self-creating and self-created, possesses infinite attributes, is the cause of all things, and is free in the sense that he acts merely according to the necessary laws of his own nature. Everything less than the single substance God or Nature is affected by causes other than itself, and the existence of anything less than God cannot be explained wholly as the effect of its own essential properties or essence; knowledge of an external cause is required for complete knowledge and explanation of any finite thing; in this sense the essence of things produced by God does not involve their existence; for it is a tautology that if they are not self-created, their existence cannot be explained by reference to their own essential attributes (*Ethics Pt.* I. *Prop.* XXIV). But, since precisely the opposite is true of God, one can say of God, and only of God, that his existence involves his essence and *vice versa;* in his case only, essence and existence are equivalent (*Ethics Pt.* I. *Prop.* XX). 'God's existence and his essence are one and the same thing' is a now unfamiliar, scholastic way of saying that to know that God exists is the same as to know what are his essential attributes, which is in turn the same as to know that he exists; that God exists is taken to follow directly from the proposition that God is the cause of himself or is self-creating. But to know the essential attributes of a triangle is not necessarily to know that there actually exist triangles possessing these attributes; in the case of triangles, or of anything other than God, knowledge of their existence necessarily involves knowledge of other things which are the causes of their existence; merely by considering the properties involved in being triangular, we cannot infer that anything actually exists possessing these properties.

It must be noticed that when God is called a free cause, 'free' must not be understood to have the meaning which it has when applied to human activities. It is a general principle in Spinoza's philosophy, which he constantly repeats to prevent misunderstandings, that no term when applied to God can possibly bear the meaning which it has when applied to human beings; he implies that it is neglect of this logically necessary principle which has produced the confusions of traditional theology. The confusion which suggests itself when God or Nature is conceived as a free and originating cause or creator is a confusion between 'free' and 'voluntary'; when we speak of human action as free, 'free' does generally mean voluntary. But it is strictly meaningless to describe God as acting either voluntarily or involuntarily; God acts or creates freely *because* he acts necessarily – 'Things could not have been produced by God in any manner or order other than that in which they were produced' (*Ethics Pt.* I. *Prop.* XXXIII). God or Nature is free because self-determined; but self-determination is incompatible with undetermined or arbitrary choice, which is the meaning often attached to 'free' in its application to human actions. This is only one example of the general principle that we must divest our psychological vocabulary – words like 'will', 'desire', 'love' – of all its customary associations and connotations, when we apply it, not, as we normally do, to a human being who is a finite and dependent being, but to God the infinite and self-determining substance. If intellect and will belong to God's eternal essence, the names of these activities cannot be here used in the sense in which men generally use them; for the intellect and will which would constitute God's essence would have to differ entirely from our intellect and will, and could resemble ours in nothing except the name.

God eternally causes all things to exist, and to possess the essential attributes which they do possess; 'God is not only the effecting cause of the existence of things, but also of their essence' (*Ethics Pt.* I. *Prop.* XXV). This proposition implies that in order to explain why things possess the properties which they actually do possess, we must ultimately exhibit their possession of such properties as deducible from the total scheme of Nature, that is, as deducible from the essential attributes and modes of God.

The traditional conception of God as the transcendent creator distinct from his creation involved Christian and Jewish philosophers (among Christians particularly Leibniz) in special problems about the limits of God's powers as creator; God is by definition omnipotent, yet there seems difficulty in describing his power as creator as unlimited; for surely his power as creator was limited by logical necessities. His choice of the actual world could not be admitted to be an altogether free choice, with the implication that all combinations of attributes were logically possible; for if the doctrine of essences or real natures is to be maintained, some attributes must be necessarily connected with others, and some must be logically incompatible with others. Therefore to those who conceived God as transcendent creator, a dilemma presented itself, a dilemma which has more than merely theological interest. Either God is conceived as *absolutely* free to create the world as he chooses: in which case the doctrine of *absolutely* immutable essences in Nature, on which the possibility of secure and adequate knowledge was conceived to rest, must be abandoned; what attributes are connected in Nature depends on God's arbitrary choice, and cannot be discovered by purely logical analysis. If this is admitted, the distinction between that which is logically necessary and that which is merely contingent ceases to be absolutely valid, since all things are ultimately contingent as the products of God's arbitrary fiat; we are left to discover what God has willed by purely experimental methods, and cannot rely on any *a priori* insight into logical necessities. Alternatively, if, like Leibniz, one wishes to maintain as far as possible the distinction between what is logically necessary and what is merely contingent in human knowledge, one must say that God was not *absolutely* free to create any world consisting of any arbitrary combination of properties, but free only to choose the best of all logically possible worlds; his choice was confined to what is logically possible and guided by a preference of the best. In order to preserve God's freedom in the creation of the world, while not excluding the possibility of a rational explanation of the order of Nature, one can say that he had sufficient reasons for choosing to create the actual world; he had reasons which *inclined* him so to choose, but did not *necessitate* his choice; other choices were logically possible. This delicate and unstable compromise was suggested by Leibniz, because he was above all concerned to reconcile, or at least to appear to reconcile, the demands of orthodox theology with the claims of rationalistic science. God created the world by a free act of will, but his creation can be understood by the exercise of reason, using the principle of non-contradiction and the principle of sufficient reason as guides in discovery.

Such speculations about the nature and limits of God's freedom in creation may now seem remote and unreal, mere metaphysical or theological quibbles without relevance to actual problems; but within these now unfamiliar theological terms the logical issue of the foundations of scientific knowledge was thinly disguised. The problem of God's causality and power is only one expression of the rationalist philosopher's problem – Can the properties of everything in Nature be represented as ultimately intelligible to human reason within a single deductive system which reflects the whole order of Nature? Or must we, at least at some points, appeal to revelation of the mysteries of God's will in order to explain things in Nature which must always be inexplicable by reason alone? This question, which was fundamental to the philosophies prescribing the early programme of natural science in the seventeenth century, is the background of Spinoza's otherwise obscure doctrine of God's immanent causality. Spinoza, as a complete rationalist, accepted without qualification the first of these alternatives, and with it all the theological consequences from which the prudent Leibniz discreetly recoiled; he thereby earned the label, superficially so absurd, of atheist. He was an atheist in the sense that he denied the possibility of a personal God who by an act of will created the Universe.

If the possibility of a Creator distinct from his Creation is denied, and God or Nature is conceived to be eternally self-creating, and free in the sense of self-determined, then it follows that 'The power of God is the same as his essence' (*Ethics Pt.* I. *Prop.* XXXIV), and that 'Things could not have been produced by God in any manner or order other than that in which they were produced' (*Ethics Pt.* I. *Prop.* XXXIII). These two propositions, taken together, are taken to be the consequences of denying the possibility of a transcendent creator; God's creation cannot be conceived as an act of will or choice, as the human builder's creation of a house is an act of will or choice. Everything in the Universe is created or produced by God in the sense, and only in the sense, that the existence and properties of everything in the Universe are deducible from an adequate knowledge of the essential and eternal attributes and modes of God's being; and this is what is meant by the sentence 'The power of God (i.e. to produce) is the same as his essence'. The created Universe (*Natura Naturata*) is the necessary expression of God's essential nature; it is meaningless to conceive God or Nature's creative power (*Natura Naturans*) as allowing the possibility of creating worlds other than the actual world; for this would be to imply that God as creative (*Natura Naturans*) is not co-extensive and identical with what is created (*Natura Naturata*). The possible cannot be wider than the actual, in the sense that the actual world is one of a number of possible worlds, as Leibniz was to hold; the actual world is the only possible world, and therefore, in any ordinary sense of choice or will, it is meaningless to conceive God as exercising choice or will in creation.

The circle of propositions and definitions which, taken together, build Spinoza's conception of the single substance, God or Nature, is so designed that, if one enters the circle at any point, one ought to be able, following an unbroken thread of logical connexion, to traverse every proposition of this part of his system and to return ultimately to one's starting point. There can therefore be as many different orders of exposition of the fundamentals of the system as there are propositions which can be taken as starting points; which proposition is best taken as starting point depends in part at least on which of the various notions involved is assumed to be the least unfamiliar and unintelligible; so one may move from the relatively evident and self-explanatory to the more obscure propositions. It is, I believe, a mistake to look for any one, or even two, propositions or definitions in Part I of the *Ethics*, which may be taken as logically prior, or as the ultimate premises from which all the others are derived. Secondly, in any such deductive system, containing terms endowed by exact definition with meanings which may be remote from their current meanings, the significance of the initial propositions can be understood only in the light of their logical consequences in the later propositions; one has to travel round the whole circle at least once before one can begin to understand any segment of it. In this chapter only a few of the possible orders of logical dependence among these basic metaphysical propositions have been exhibited. It is enough if the logical interdependence of the propositions is clear, with the effect that the reader does not have the impression that he could easily accept part of Spinoza's metaphysics and reject the rest. At least the metaphysics ought to be admitted to be a system, even if it is in the end to be rejected just because it is a metaphysical system.

The larger question of assessing the adequacy of this first part of Spinoza's system must be postponed until its consequences have been explained.

THE INFINITE ATTRIBUTES

'By "attribute" I mean that which intellect perceives as constituting the essential nature of substance' (*Ethics Pt.* I. *Def.* IV). 'Each attribute of the one substance must be conceived through itself' (*Ethics Pt.* I. *Prop.* X). 'God or a substance consisting of infinite attributes, each of which expresses eternal and infinite essence, necessarily exists' (*Ethics Pt.* I. *Prop.* XI).

The unique substance which is God or Nature has been shown to be all-inclusive or infinite, and God's essential nature cannot in principle be conceived as exhausted in any finite list of attributes. To conceive God or Nature as all-inclusive and infinite is the same, in Spinoza's language, as to conceive God as possessing infinite attributes. The attributes of substance or God are simply the essential nature of God as conceived by the intellect, and are called 'attributes' because to conceive God or substance intellectually is to 'attribute' such and such a nature to God or substance (*Letter* IX). But as God's essential nature is infinite, there is an infinity of ways in which he can be conceived by the intellect, and therefore there must be allowed to be an infinity of attributes. Secondly, each attribute, being the essential nature of God or substance as it presents itself to the intellect, is itself infinite; if it were not infinite in its own kind, it could not be an expression of the essential nature of God. Therefore one is compelled to speak of an infinity of attributes, each of which is in itself infinite.

This doctrine of infinite attributes immediately perplexed Spinoza's friends and has perplexed all subsequent commentators. The obscurity can be partly (perhaps not entirely) relieved by insisting on the peculiarities of his semi-scholastic vocabulary, which is so easily misinterpreted and mistranslated. Within this vocabulary to conceive, or think about (not imagine), God or Nature is to conceive a substance as possessing some attribute. Since all propositions are assumed to attribute a predicate to a subject, this is no more than to say that to think about God or Nature is to entertain some proposition of which God or Nature is the subject. Any proposition of which God is the subject is either self-contradictory or necessarily true, that is, such that its denial is self-contradictory. It follows that we cannot deny that God possesses any attribute, or make God the subject of any negative proposition, unless we mean to say that the possession of one attribute is incompatible with the possession of some other attribute. God possesses all positive attributes, or is perfect, because of any list of attributes it is impossible to say that these are the *only* attributes which God possesses; for to say this would be to make God the subject of a simple negative proposition. However the intellect may conceive God and with whatever propositions we may describe God's power and activity, we can never say that these propositions exhaust God's power, or that God cannot be conceived in any other way. We cannot make any such simple negative statements about that which is all-inclusive and infinite, since we would thereby be setting limits to God's power or perfection.

Although we cannot set limits to the way in which God might in principle be conceived by the intellect, we find, when we analyse the notion of Nature as the totality of things, that we can think of Nature as a physical system, or system of things extended in space, and also as a system of minds or thoughts. Extension and thought are the two all-pervasive characteristics of the self-creating Universe as it actually presents itself to the limited human intellect. The Universe can be conceived either as a system of extended bodies, an infinite spatial system, or as a system of thought; both conceptions of the Universe are complete in themselves, but one is not reducible to the other; we cannot conceive thought as a modification of extension, or extension as a modification of thought. This doctrine, which is (and will always remain) difficult to understand, is certainly worth understanding, if only because from it are deduced some of the most lucid and practical of Spinoza's suggestions in psychology and ethics; and, freely interpreted, it is very relevant to what are still some of the central problems of natural philosophy. But it cannot be understood without some reference to Descartes, from whom this distinction between Thought and Extension is derived.

EXTENSION

Everyone distinguishes in some rough way between the physical and the mental, between bodies and minds.

Descartes laid emphasis on this distinction in order to mark as clearly as possible the scope and limits of the new mathematical science, which would be concerned wholly with the measurable properties of bodies in space. Nature was therefore divided into Extension, the system described in mathematical physics, and the realm of Thought, which cannot be so described. In Descartes' philosophy Extension and Thought are two self-contained and independent systems. Extension can be roughly (but not exactly) equated with the system of what are ordinarily called physical objects, the world of objects occupying some position in space. But of a mind or a mental event it is meaningless to ask 'Where is it?' or to attribute any spatial relations or properties to it. My mind, as opposed to the physical object which is my brain, is not literally 'inside my head', and my thoughts, unlike my brain, cannot be said to occupy any position in space. Descartes' distinction between Extension and Thought accurately underlines at least one of the distinctions generally implied in ordinary usage when we distinguish between what is physical and what is mental; in ordinary usage to classify an event as a physical event is generally equivalent to saying that it occupies some position in space, and to classify an event as a mental event is equivalent to saying that it does not occupy a position in space. By an extended thing Descartes means a thing having spatial properties, and by extension, abstractly conceived, the whole actual system of space and spatial relations which constitutes what is ordinarily called the physical world. Descartes himself made an original contribution to analytical geometry, and his whole philosophy, and particularly the conception of the physical world as extension, was designed to point the way to a new physical science expressed in geometrical terms; within this science the properties of things, and the laws governing their movements and changes of state, were to be expressed in purely mathematical terms, excluding mention of qualities of colour, taste, and sound, in so far as colour, taste, and sound are not as such directly measurable. The changing properties of objects are to be expressed as changes of configuration within the single spatial system, so that within optics, for instance, changes of colour became measurable changes of light rays impinging on the retina; the qualitative differences of our sensations are to be replaced in the scientific description by the quantitative changes on which they depend.

This reformed physical science expressed in geometrical terms was taken to be in principle inapplicable to the workings of a mind; it seemed that the mental or non-spatial world could not be described and understood in these terms, and must be conceived as a wholly separate and distinct compartment of reality; it seemed as if the world must be conceived as divisible into two compartments, which are mutually exclusive and which do not overlap; for neither world can be described or explained in terms which are appropriate to the other. Descartes so emphasized the distinction between the two compartments of reality, Extension and Thought, that they were each conceived as substances or quasi-substances in the strict sense of the word; changes or modifications of the extended world are only to be fully and properly explained in terms of the properties of extension. There could in principle be no necessary connexion, intelligible in the light of reason alone, between the world of extended things and the world of thought, that is, no necessary connexion of the kind which exists *within* the world of extended things; it is a fact that changes in the world of thought produce, or lead to, changes in extended things, and we may control our bodies and passions by will and rational choice. But we cannot deduce, and in this strict sense explain, the physical changes as the necessary consequences of the mental, as we can explain one physical change as the necessary consequence of another; the connexion between the two realms remains in this sense impenetrable to our reason.

It must be admitted that many reflective and unreflective people have conceived minds and bodies as constituting two essentially different realms or orders of being, neither of which can be explained in terms of the other; and many people are alarmed, and many more were alarmed in earlier ages of faith, by the apparent theological and moral consequences of not maintaining some such rigid distinction between the physical and the mental worlds. But the philosophical or logical difficulties which are involved in pressing the ordinary distinction as far as Descartes pressed it are very great, and are shown very clearly in the embarrassed history of Cartesianism after Descartes; it is these difficulties which Spinoza drastically overcomes. Spinoza's doctrine of the all-inclusive self-creating God or Nature rested on what he believed to be the logical impossibility of conceiving the Universe, as Descartes had conceived it, as consisting of *two* self-contained systems; and he could have pointed to the famous embarrassment of Descartes himself, and even more of followers such as Malebranche, as evidence, if evidence were needed, of the impossibility of maintaining such a dualism. Unfortunately he does not himself explain how his own metaphysic arises naturally and necessarily from considering the incoherences in Descartes; the transition can be reconstructed, but is left implicit in the *Ethics*.

Any two-substance doctrine, representing the spatial world and the world of thought as independent and self-contained systems, must obviously be embarrassed in describing human personality; for one ordinarily thinks of a person as essentially consisting of a mind and a body, each causally related to the other in some very intimate way. As Descartes allows, one naturally thinks of events in my mind causing events in my body (e.g. a sudden decision causing a movement of muscles), and of bodily events causing mental events (e.g. a blow causing a sensation of pain); one does not ordinarily suppose that all states of my body could be explained without reference to states of my mind or *vice versa*. In ordinary thought and language mind and body are represented as interacting, and the modifications of each are ordinarily explained, at least in part, by reference to the modifications of the other.

But to conceive thought and extension as two substances is logically to preclude the possibility of strictly causal interaction between them in the old rationalist sense of 'cause'; a change in the world of extended things cannot be the cause of a change in thought, at least in the sense in which one modification of extension may be the cause of another modification of extension. Descartes met this difficulty partly by a rather lame appeal to a special hypothesis in physiology, partly by accepting the causal relation between the world of thought and the world of extended things as a mystery which cannot in principle be made entirely intelligible to human reason. Malebranche, writing after Descartes, suggested that the correlation between physical and mental changes should be described, not by saying that one might be the cause of another, but that one might be the 'occasion' of another; this phrase was explicitly, and gratefully, admitted to conceal a mystery of divine creation, not penetrable by human reason; God is required perpetually to intervene to maintain the order of natural events. Spinoza, a rationalist without reservation, allowed no appeals to God's inscrutable will or to theological mysteries in the design of his metaphysics. He therefore argued that the two pervasive features of the Universe as it presents itself to our minds, the Universe as a system of extended or spatial things and the Universe as a system of ideas or thought, must be interpreted as two aspects of a single inclusive reality; they are not to be conceived as two distinct substances, a conception which has been proved to be self-contradictory; they must be two attributes of the single substance.

It follows that the whole system, which is God or Nature, can be conceived equally, and no less completely, as a system of extended or spatial things or as a system of thinking or animated things; everything extended in space is also truly conceived as animated, and everything animated is also truly conceived as extended in space. In order to appreciate Spinoza's intention, it is essential from the beginning not to attach to the infinite attributes of Thought and Extension only the ordinary associations of the words mind and body; for the attributes of Thought and Extension are not in Spinoza two partly parallel, or somehow co-ordinated, systems of things or events, as mental and physical events are ordinarily imagined to be. They are the same order of causes in the same substance, but conceived under two different attributes of this substance. Thinking substance and extended substance are one and the same substance, comprehended now under this attribute, now under that ... 'Whether we think of Nature under the attribute of Extension or under the attribute of Thought or under any other attribute whatever, we shall discover one and the same order, or one and the same connexion of causes' (*Ethics Pt.* II. *Prop.* VII. *Note*). The union of individual human minds with individual human bodies is for Spinoza only a special case of the general identity of the order or connexion of causes in Nature; what he has proved refers no more to man than to other individual things, all of which are, though in different degrees, animate. '*For of everything there is necessarily an idea in God, of which God is the cause, in the same way as there is an idea of the human body* [the italics are mine]: thus whatever we have asserted of the idea of the human body must necessarily also be asserted of the idea of everything else. But still we cannot deny that ideas, like objects, differ one from the other, one being more excellent than the other and containing more reality, just as the object of one idea is more excellent than the object of another idea, and contains more reality' (*Ethics Pt.* II. *Prop.* XIII. *Note*). This passage explains Spinoza's intention, which has been persistently misinterpreted because of a too simple equation of his thought and extension with the mental and physical, as this distinction is ordinarily understood. He is asserting that, since there are both extended things and ideas of extended things, as Nature presents itself to us, and since both the extended things and the ideas must belong to the unique self-determining substance, there can be no ideas which are not ideas of extended things, or extended things of which there is no idea.

From his conception of the unique substance and its attributes, Spinoza is deducing that the system of ideas which constitutes God, as conceived under the attribute of thought, must not only correspond to, but coincide with, the objects of these ideas, their *ideata;* he is showing that, if God is rightly conceived as the unique substance, the problem which confronted Descartes – how can we be certain that our clear and distinct ideas correspond to reality? – cannot even arise; there can be no question of

the *correspondence* between the order of thought or ideas
and the order of things, because there are not *two* orders
to correspond. So the doctrine of the two Infinite attributes
of God or Nature leads to what is the most economical and
complete of all the many philosopher's proofs that the real
is the rational, or, in Spinoza's terminology, that *ideata*
and ideas coincide. Descartes, starting from a dualism
which separates minds or thinking things and their ideas
from the extra-mental or extended world, had needed once
again to appeal to a transcendent God to guarantee that our
thoughts, rightly ordered, can be assumed to correspond
to reality; before it can be proved that our ideas correspond to reality, and therefore before it can be proved
that real knowledge is accessible to us, we must first prove
that God exists and is not a deceiver. Critics of Descartes
have always remarked that this procedure appears circular,
since we apparently require to have made the last step in
the proof before we are justified in making the first; we
cannot be certain beyond doubt that our clear and distinct
ideas are true, until we have proved the existence of God;
but – it will be suggested – we cannot prove the existence
of God without first assuming that our clear and distinct
ideas are true. Spinoza is logically entitled to take it for
granted from the beginning that the order of our thoughts
and judgements must always reflect the order of actual
physical events or things; for his doctrine of the single
substance conceived under two attributes implies that there
can be no idea without something extended of which it is
the idea, and there can be no extended thing of which there

is no idea. It follows that to trace the hierarchy of ideas from the most confused and inadequate up to the most clear and adequate, as in the theory of knowledge, is at the same time to investigate the hierarchy of things, from the finite and perishing things up to the infinite and eternal order of Nature, as in metaphysics. This is the key to Spinoza's method in his moral theory and throughout his writing. Corresponding to each level of knowledge or type of idea there is an *ideatum* of the same degree of reality; degrees of rationality and degrees of reality must in this sense be linked at every stage. It follows that, in so far as we so purify our understanding as to entertain only ideas of the highest order of rationality, we must approximate to the condition of God, and to that extent we cease to be subordinate parts of Nature; our status as natural objects wholly depends on the type of idea which constitutes our minds, and the type of idea which constitutes our minds wholly depends on our status as natural objects; and this, and (I think) only this, is what is meant by the paradoxical statement that all things are in their different degrees animated. Spinoza is not saying that all things have minds, in the popular sense in which human beings are said to have minds; it follows only that for every extended thing there is an idea of that thing, and in the special case of a human body, the idea is a human mind. The paradox arises from Spinoza's peculiar interpretation of the union of personal minds and bodies, by which a human body is the *ideatum* of which the animating mind is the idea; he makes the union of mind and body which constitutes a person only a special case of the general principle of the coincidence of ideas and their *ideata;* and he thereby suggests an interpretation of the mind-body relationship which has always interested philosophers, even when they have rejected the rest of his metaphysics.

MIND AND BODY

For every body in nature there exists an idea of that body; for every triangular figure there exists an idea of that figure. Similarly, for everything which would ordinarily be called a human body, there exists an idea of that body, and such an idea is what is ordinarily called a human mind. Every modification of, or change of state in, a human body necessarily involves, in view of the identity of the order of causes within the two attributes, a modification of the idea of that body, and so involves a modification of the mind. A human mind has greater or less power and perfection in so far as the body, of which it is the idea, has greater power and perfection; the converse must also be true. Below human beings in the scale of power and perfection come animals, and the idea of an animal's body is not ordinarily said to constitute a mind. But the difference is one of degree of complication in structure and organization. An animal has less power and perfection than a human being, in the sense that there are fewer things which it can do; the range of its reactions is narrower; at some levels of experience the human mind, and therefore the human body, may sink to the animal level, the range of action and reaction becoming no greater than an animal's. In so far as the order of ideas which constitutes my mind approximates to the order of ideas which constitutes the infinite attribute of thought in God or Nature, my mind may be said to approximate to God's mind; to that degree of approximation my mind may be said to reflect the whole order of Nature. But of course no human mind can ever reflect the whole order of Nature, and so attain absolutely perfect knowledge; for this would necessarily involve the human body becoming identical with infinite extension. We must ascend or descend the scale between the animal and the divine as whole persons; it is only Cartesian dualism which leads us to talk as if our mental development might be independent of our physical development. Human beings are, in the popular phrase, parts of Nature, but they may be more or less subordinate parts, the degree of subordination depending upon the different degrees of development of the power of their minds-and-bodies, of their whole personality.

EXTENSION AND ITS MODES

Everything which exists in the Universe is to be conceived as a 'modification' or particular differentiation of the unique, all-inclusive substance, whose nature is revealed to us solely under the two infinite attributes, Thought and Extension. But we can and must distinguish the all-pervasive features of the Universe, which can be immediately deduced from the nature of these attributes themselves, from those which cannot be so immediately deduced. The modes or features of Reality which seem essential to the constitution of these two infinite and eternal attributes must themselves be infinite and eternal; they are therefore distinguished by Spinoza as the immediate infinite and eternal modes, the word 'mode' being used for anything which is a state of substance. The modes or states of substance can be graded in an order of logical dependence, beginning with the immediate infinite and eternal modes as necessary and universal features of the Universe, and descending to the finite modes which are limited, perishing and transitory differentiations of Nature. The transitory, finite modes can only be understood, and their essence or nature deduced, as effects of the infinite and eternal modes, and they are in this sense dependent on the modes of higher order. The infinite and eternal mode under the attribute of Extension is called Motion-and-Rest. To understand the significance of this phrase one must again refer to Descartes' unsolved metaphysical difficulties, which were always a deciding influence in the formation of Spinoza's doctrines. Descartes' conception of the physical world as Extension had left physical change or motion accounted for as the effect of the creator's will; God, who was transcendent and external to the world he had created, had implanted motion in it. Spinoza, having rejected the notion of a creator external to his own creation as being self-contradictory, is once again in the situation of representing as a necessary feature of Nature, and as immanent in the system, what Descartes had represented as a fiat of God's will. If the hypothesis of a transcendent God implanting motion in the system of extended bodies is impossible, then it will be an intrinsic characteristic of the extended or spatial world that everything within it is constituted of particular proportions of motion and rest; motion will be essential to, and inseparable from, the nature and constitution of extended things. The proportions of motion and rest within the system as a whole will be constant, since there can be no external cause to explain any change in the system; but within the subordinate parts of the system the proportions of motion and rest are constantly changing in the interaction of these parts among each other.

It seems natural to translate the now unfamiliar phrase 'Motion-and-Rest' as 'energy'; one can then represent Spinoza as in effect saying that the extended world is to be conceived as a self-contained, and all-inclusive, system of interactions in which the total amount of energy is constant; and, secondly, he is in effect saying that all the changing qualities and configurations of extended bodies can be adequately represented solely as transmissions or exchanges of energy within this single system. Spinoza's denial that an act of creation by a transcendent creator is logically possible could be translated as a denial of the possibility of energy entering into the system from outside; the physical world must be conceived as complete in itself, self-generating and self-maintaining. Commentators have generally remarked that Spinoza, in making motion-and-rest the fundamental concept to be used in describing the spatial or physical world, in fact anticipated more closely than Descartes the future structure of mathematical physics; he seems to have envisaged physical explanation as being necessarily dynamical in form, with physical things represented as ultimately no more than configurations of force and energy. But it must be remembered that such interpretations, although incidentally illuminating, are not to be taken as direct and literal translations; for concepts such as force and energy, as they occur in modern physical theories, are not metaphysical concepts; they can ultimately be interpreted, however indirectly, in terms of equations verified by actual experiments and observations. Spinoza is deducing the necessity of motion-and-rest as a primary characteristic of the extended world without any reference to convenience in summarizing actual experimental results; he is appealing only to the strictly logical implications of his prior notions of a self-creating substance conceived as an extended thing (*res extensa*). But the deductive system which is his metaphysics is so much the more worth studying if, following its own logic, it results in a programme of scientific explanation which in outline accords with the actual methods of later science. This is certainly one of the tests of the adequacy of a metaphysical system.

Within the single system of extension, what we normally single out as particular physical bodies or things owe their identity and their distinguishing characteristics to the particular proportion of motion and rest among the ultimate or elementary particles (*corpora simpliccisma*) of which they are composed. What we normally call particular things or bodies are to be analysed into configurations of ultimate particles. Those changes of quality in the gross composite bodies, to which we refer in ordinary language, are to be conceived scientifically as changes in the velocity and cohesion of the elementary particles. Qualitative changes in medium-sized objects, as these are described in common-sense knowledge, are represented in the light of systematic knowledge solely as measurable changes in the velocity and configuration of qualitatively undifferentiated particles. Like Descartes and other natural philosophers after Galileo, Spinoza regarded all change in the qualities of things as properly to be described in purely quantitative terms; this was the necessary faith or methodological assumption of the new mathematical physics which they planned; this was to be the great discovery of the century, one that was supposedly ignored or not fully understood by Bacon and other empiricists. The changing colours and sounds to which we refer in the language of common-sense are properly described in terms of light-rays and vibrations, and these in turn are ultimately explained (by Spinoza) as exchanges of energy among elementary particles; this was the programme which in metaphysics could be expressed by saying that only the primary or measurable properties of things are real. The physical objects referred to in our ordinary language, including the human body, are all, when properly conceived in the language of science, shown to be elaborately complex bodies, though of different orders of complexity; they may be not first-order configurations of elementary particles, but configurations of configurations of configurations ... up to any order of complexity. As long as within any configuration constituting a physical thing the total amount of motion-and-rest within the configuration as a whole remains roughly constant, the physical object retains its nature or identity, however much the distribution of motion-and-rest (or energy) between different parts of the configuration may have changed; the change of distribution of proportions of motion-and-rest within the configuration accounts for, or is the real equivalent of, what we ordinarily call the changing qualities of the object. Following this method of analysis, which allows us to regard any more or less stable configuration, although internally complex and sub-divisible into further configurations, as a single individual, 'We may (to quote Spinoza), if we go on *ad infinitum*, conceive the whole of Nature as one individual, the parts of which (that is to say, all bodies) change in infinite ways, without any change of the whole individual' (*Ethics Pt.* II. *Lem. VII. Note*). This highest-order individual Spinoza calls 'the face of the whole Universe' (*facies totius Universi*); in the hierarchy of his system of modes, it has the title of 'a mediate infinite and eternal mode' under the attribute of extension. It is 'mediate' because it is logically dependent on the immediate mode of motion-and-rest, which is the primary, or logically prior, feature of extension; it is 'infinite' and 'eternal', because the fact that Nature as a whole, conceived as a spatial system, remains thus self-identical follows directly from the conception of motion-and-rest as the necessary feature of the extended world.

Particular things or bodies, objects in the ordinary sense, can be no more than finite modes; that they are finite follows directly from their status as sub-systems within the total system; they are finite in the sense that they are not all-inclusive but are bounded by other objects within the system, the infinite being by definition the all-inclusive; they cannot be eternal, but must come into being and pass away as the distribution of proportions of motion and rest within the universe changes. Any finite thing within Nature is constantly being affected by other finite causes in its environment, and by those restless transmissions of motion to its parts which constitute change within the universe; the history of any particular thing, or finite mode, is the history of its constant interaction with its environment, of 'being affected in many ways', while sufficiently maintaining that internal cohesion which depends on the relative constancy of balance of motion-and-rest within it. The more complex the particular thing is, that is, the more configurations it contains, the greater the variety of ways in which it can affect and be affected by its environment. On this scale of complexity, and therefore on this scale of power to affect and be affected by its environment, the human body must come very high among natural objects, with animals and so-called inanimate objects lower in the scale. The human body, therefore, is in this sense 'more excellent and contains more reality' than animal or vegetable bodies; and 'to contain more reality' means to possess more power. That relatively very complex system, the human body, is affected in a greater variety of ways by its environment, and so reflects the order of causes in nature more fully than do animal or vegetable bodies. Therefore the idea of which a human body is the *ideatum*, and which is a human mind, is also 'more excellent and contains more reality', and must reflect a relatively wider range of causes in the Universe. The difference between a finite mode which is a human mind-body and a finite mode which is an animal is entirely a difference of degree of complexity; although any finite mode of Extension can be said to 'have a soul' (*anima*) in the unfamiliar sense that there necessarily exists an idea of that mode under the attribute of thought, only of human bodies do we say that the idea of them is a mind (*mens*). Spinoza, like Descartes, showed an unsentimental and un-English disregard of the soulfulness of animals; they both held that we are entirely justified in exploiting them for our own purposes.

Each particular thing, interacting with other particular things within the common order of Nature, exhibits a characteristic tendency to cohesion and to the preservation of its identity, a 'striving (*conatus*), so far as it lies in itself to do so, to persist in its own being' (*Ethics Pt. III. Prop. VII*). This striving towards cohesion and the preservation of its own identity constitutes the essence of any particular thing, in the only sense in which particular things, which are not substances, can be said to have essences. Particular things, being dependent modes and not substances, are constantly undergoing changes of state as the effects of causes other than themselves; as they are not self-determining substances, their successive states cannot be deduced from their own essence alone, but must be explained partly by reference to the action upon them of other particular things. Each particular thing possesses a determinate nature of its own only in so far as it is active and not passive in relation to things other than itself, that is, only in so far as its states can be explained otherwise than as the effects of external causes; only so far as a thing is an originating cause – and clearly a dependent mode cannot be entirely an originating cause – can any individuality, any determinate nature of its own, be attributed to it. Its character and individuality depends on its necessarily limited power of self-maintenance; it can be distinguished as a unitary thing with a recognizable constancy of character in so far as, although a system of parts, it succeeds in maintaining its own characteristic coherence and balance of parts.

The importance of this doctrine of *conatus*, the striving towards self-maintenance of all particular things within the common order of Nature, is that it qualifies what would otherwise seem a too crudely mechanical or atomistic account of the physical world. It implies that our ordinary distinctions of sub-systems within the single physical system of Nature do have some justification in reality, although these sub-systems are never to be represented as genuinely independent substances; for this would imply that their states can be understood without reference to the order of causes in the all-inclusive system. Spinoza, being like Descartes largely pre-occupied with the possibilities of a systematic physics, might otherwise seem to have provided for no distinction in kind between composite objects which are organisms and composite objects which are pure machines, or even between living and non-living systems. In his natural philosophy the differences between the living and the non-living, and between conscious and unconscious things, are both represented as differences of degree of structural complication; the development of all finite modes of extension must be explained ultimately in purely physical terms, that is, in terms of exchanges of energy among groups of elementary particles. But the notion of *conatus*, or individual self-maintenance, of which there is no equivalent in Descartes or in purely mechanical and atomistic cosmologies, is exactly the concept which biologists have often demanded as essential to the understanding of organic and living systems. It is characteristic of Spinoza that he extends this principle of the relative unity of particular things, and of the differentiation among them, to all levels of organization, and applies it to the simplest mechanical systems as well as to organic and living systems; for he is throughout providing for a unitary method of scientific explanation. But he can also allow that in the higher-order systems, which consist of configurations within configurations through many levels, the relative cohesion, or tendency to self-maintenance, in spite of internal change is the more noticeable, precisely because of the greater possible variety of internal change; in the study of organic systems, and even more in the study of living systems, the contrast between internal diversity, arising out of the constant dissolution and replacement of sub-systems, and the persisting equilibrium and self-maintenance of the whole, is much more conspicuous.

It must again be noticed how astonishingly Spinoza, in his modal system of extension, has anticipated in outline the concepts and theoretical methods of modern science. If (as is sometimes suggested) metaphysical systems or cosmologies are to be judged as programmes or drafts in outline of the structure of a future science, it is not too much to claim that Spinoza, at least in his account of Nature as Extension, was less incomplete in his anticipations than any other philosopher; certainly he was less incomplete in his anticipations than Descartes. It was not until the end of the last century that his three conceptions (*a*) of motion-and-rest as the essential and universal feature of the extended world, and (*b*) of ultimate particles as centres of energy, and (*c*) of configurations of these ultimate particles forming relatively self-maintaining systems, were seen to correspond with actually used scientific concepts. In the two hundred years' interval, cruder conceptions of 'matter' as a homogeneous, solid stuff, or the more simple atomic hypothesis of Gassendi and others, were the popularly accepted metaphysical background of physical science; such crude conceptions of matter provide an imaginative picture or model of the physical world which is more easily understood. In the last century Spinoza was sometimes celebrated, and much more often abominated, as a precursor of materialism; but his was a materialism with a difference, if only because the word 'matter' normally suggests something solid and inert, and no such notion of matter is to be found in his writing. But, what is more important, both crude materialism and Descartes' mathematical system of Extension seem to take no account of the development of the biological sciences, or of those points of contact between biology and physics, which in this century have become of the greatest philosophical interest. Spinoza, because, unlike Descartes, he designed a single system of concepts to apply over the whole range of the natural world, did anticipate these interests in outline; he did not think of knowledge as divisible into unrelated compartments. The actually used distinction between the lowest forms of living systems and the most highly organized forms of matter closely corresponds to Spinoza's distinction between systems persisting through relatively greater exchanges of energy with their environment (e.g. in respiration), as opposed to systems which exhibit less internal change; and these distinctions are generally recognized in practice as distinctions of degrees of organization, which are not in themselves of any ultimate theoretical importance; they are no longer thought of as theoretically irreducible distinctions, which correspond to some ultimate difference in the nature of the substances investigated. By Descartes such a structure as the human brain was still represented as a machine; but Spinoza, with his model of systems within systems each with its own characteristic equilibrium of forces, analysed the nature and stressed the importance of complications of structure of a different degree. His picture is so much the less crudely mechanical and so much closer to modern biology and physics. After Descartes had taken the first great step within natural philosophy towards a unitary physics by breaking down the Aristotelian division of the world into natural kinds, Spinoza took an equally large step towards the project of a single system of organized knowledge when he challenged the last remaining division of reality into two irreducibly separate compartments, somehow causally related – the mental and the physical. The two attributes are still regarded as irreducible one to the other: but, as they are two attributes under which a single substance is conceived, the connexion between them must be more intimate than any causal connexion could be. The necessity of a one-to-one correspondence between the order of ideas and the order of extended things is a purely *logical* necessity, which requires no further guarantee. Any philosopher who questions what has been called the official Two-world doctrine formulated by Descartes is liable to be classified as a materialist, even if he is simply rejecting the conception of minds and bodies as constituting two independent systems, each a realm in itself. Spinoza was certainly not a materialist in the other and cruder sense; he never tried to represent minds or persons as no more than machines, nor did he attach any meaning to 'matter' as the ultimate 'stuff' of which the Universe is made; and his metaphysics of the mind, which provides his scheme or outline of a science of psychology, was certainly not simply mechanical or behaviouristic.

CHAPTER THREE

Knowledge and Intellect

I WILL first recapitulate in order to place Spinoza's theory of knowledge in the framework of his metaphysics.

Descartes had conceived reality as divided into the two causally independent compartments of Thought and Extension. Within the world of thought he conceived a human mind as 'a created thinking substance' (*substantia cogitans creata*); an individual mind is a 'thinking thing' (*ens cogitans*). That part of my mind which is my intellect, unlike my body which is only a perishing part of the single system of Extension, is essentially independent of all changes in the universe; it is immortal; however my mere desires and feelings may change in correspondence with the changes in the states of my body, my active intellect persists unaffected by any changes in the world of things extended in space. Spinoza's theory of the mind, rigorously deduced from the conception of Nature as an indivisible whole, is developed in almost exact antithesis to Descartes'.

A human mind cannot be a created substance, since the notion of a created substance is demonstrably a self-contradiction. An individual human mind is only a particular modification of God or Nature's infinite power of thought;

in his own words, 'the human mind is part of the infinite intellect of God' (*Ethics Pt.* II. *Prop.* XI. *Coroll.*). An individual human mind is constituted by that set of ideas whose objects or *ideata* are states of an individual human body; the individual human body, as a finite mode of extension, is constantly being affected by other bodies external to it, and these effects are necessarily reflected in the ideas of the body which constitute the mind. So far from being a substance with a continuing activity normally independent of the body, my mind is the expression in idea of the successive states of my body; there is necessarily the same connexion of causes in the mind as in the body, since my mind is the idea of my body. Spinoza is not asserting the familiar doctrine that every bodily change *produces* a mental change, or that the states of my mind are causally dependent on the states of my body; he is asserting that every bodily change *is* a mental change and *vice versa*, since there is only one Nature, and one order of natural events or causes, which expresses itself, or is conceived by us, under the two Attributes. This virtual identification of bodily and mental change must seem paradoxical; as Spinoza himself repeatedly admits in the *Ethics*, it involves a drastic revision of ordinary language. Descartes' conception of the mind as an independent substance does in fact formalize the natural imagery imbedded in our language; we do ordinarily imagine the mind as some kind of immaterial substance mysteriously lodged within the body. Spinoza later tries to show why we imagine our minds as independent substances and how the superstitions imbedded in ordinary language arise from ignorance and unscientific thinking. As soon as we free ourselves from these habits of imagination, we can be led to acknowledge, by a train of deductive reasoning in the analysis of the notions of substance and cause, that this dualism, like all such dualisms, inevitably leads to contradictions. To establish that a philosophical doctrine is paradoxical, and that it involves using familiar words in unfamiliar ways, is not for Spinoza a refutation of the doctrine; it is certain *a priori* that any clear and consistent thinking must lead to conclusions which are in conflict with ordinary usage; for ordinary language necessarily reflects the confused ideas of the imagination, and not the logically coherent ideas of the intellect.

My mind, as the idea of my body, reflects the order of causes, not in Nature as a whole, but in one particular fragment of Nature; if my mind reflected the order of causes in Nature as a whole, it would be identical with God's mind and my body would be correspondingly identical with the whole of Extended Nature. The particular finite mode of Extension which is my body interacts, or exchanges energy with, its environment, and every such interaction is reflected in an idea; changes of state, which are the effects of the impinging of external bodies on the particular finite mode which is my body, are reflected in ideas which are ideas of imagination; such ideas represent the lowest level of human knowledge. In so far as my mind consists of such ideas of the imagination or of 'vague experience' (*experientia vaga*), it is said to be passive, not active; for the idea does not primarily reflect an activity of mine, and is not the effect of a sequence of previous ideas in my mind, but is primarily the effect of external causes acting on me. The level of knowledge or awareness which Spinoza calls imagination or 'confused experience' corresponds roughly to knowledge derived from sense-perception, and (at an even lower level) to the entertaining of images in dreaming and musing. In the situation which is ordinarily described as my perceiving an object, a modification of my body is occurring, which is necessarily reflected in an idea; this idea, which constitutes part of my mind at that moment, has as its object (*ideatum*) a modification, of which both the state of my body and the state of the perceived object are causes. Therefore this idea of 'confused experience' represents neither the true nature and essence of my body nor the true nature of the external object; it simply represents a particular modification of extension, without reflecting in itself the true causes of this modification. This is Spinoza's peculiar version of the ancient doctrine of rationalist philosophers that knowledge wholly derived from sense-perception is not genuine knowledge, but is in some sense subjective and uncertain. Following Plato and the rationalist tradition, he distinguishes in the *Ethics* three levels of knowledge – four are distinguished in the earlier *Treatise on the Correction of the Understanding*; knowledge wholly derived from sense-perception is assigned to the lowest level (*cognitio primi generis*), and (in the Platonic tradition) is called 'opinion'. But although the conclusion itself is traditional, it is deduced as a necessary consequence of his definition of the mind as the idea of the body, in conjunction with the usual premise that only logically necessary propositions represent genuine knowledge.

In so far as we are not engaged in pure thought, our mental life is a succession of ideas reflecting the successive modifications of the body in its interaction with other bodies, these ideas being logically unrelated to each other. Because such a sequence of ideas is never a logical sequence, sense-perception can never yield genuine knowledge; for genuine or certain knowledge is by definition a set or sequence of ideas each one of which follows logically from its predecessor. The word 'idea' is used so widely in Spinoza as to include what we would normally call an 'assertion' or 'proposition'; deliberately, and in opposition to Descartes, he makes no distinction between 'having an idea' and 'asserting' or 'making a statement'. So an idea in his sense may be qualified as true or false, and one idea may be said to follow logically from another; in normal usage we speak only of propositions or assertions as true or false, or as following logically from each other. In Spinoza's usage the idea, whose *ideatum* is some modification of my body in interaction with another body, includes what would ordinarily be called a perceptual judgement about the external body. Our ordinary perceptual judgements, which are ideas of the imagination, are not in themselves false, if considered one by one; nor can any of our perceptions be said to be in themselves absolutely illusory. There is no sense allowed in Spinoza in which any judgement or idea, *considered in isolation from other judgements or ideas*, could be said to be *absolutely* false; for, given the doctrine of the two infinite Attributes, every idea or judgement must have its *ideatum*, and therefore no question of an idea utterly failing to correspond to some independent reality can possibly arise. Spinoza emphasizes more than once that the reader must resist the tendency, arising from the ordinary associations of the word, to think of 'ideas' as 'lifeless pictures' which, if true, *correspond* to something. He admits that it is difficult to resist this habitual association of the word and he himself uses the word 'agreement' (*convenientia*) to distinguish the truth of an idea from its adequacy; and I have myself sometimes for brevity written of ideas as 'reflecting' modifications of the body. But it must always be remembered that to describe an idea as true is never in Spinoza merely to say that it corresponds to, or is a picture of, some external object or event; for all adequate ideas are true, and all true ideas are adequate; adequacy is both a necessary and sufficient condition of truth. It is the first principle of his logic, a principle which is directly deducible from the theory of the single substance conceived under two Attributes, that to say of an idea that it is true cannot be merely to say that it corresponds to any external reality; to say of an idea that it is true must be to state its relation to other ideas in the system of ideas which constitutes God's thinking. When an idea of the imagination, or an ordinary perceptual judgement, is rejected as false, this implies, in Spinoza's terminology, that that idea or judgement does not fit into a system or cohere with other ideas or judgements; it can be rejected as relatively false, that is, as false in relation to a more coherent system of ideas, which more adequately represent the order of things.

Having an illusion or hallucination, or simply making a mistake in some perceptual judgement, is for Spinoza having ideas which are even less coherent with the whole system of ideas than is normal even at the level of imagination. When we dismiss our experiences in dreams as unreal and the judgements which we make in dreams as false, we can only mean that they do not cohere with our other ideas of the imagination, even to the extent to which these ideas cohere with each other. But all perceptual judgements, even those which for normal practical purposes are described as true, are comparatively fragmentary and disconnected, and do not constitute a logically coherent system; the ideas of the imagination are, in comparison with the ideas of the pure intellect, *relatively* incoherent and unsystematic, just as what we ordinarily call false judgements of perception are relatively incoherent when compared with what are ordinarily called true perceptual judgements. It is therefore, in a sense, misleading to describe our ordinary common-sense statements about the world simply as false; they are not false in any absolute sense, since no idea or judgement is false in any absolute sense; an idea or judgement can only be described as false by comparison with some more logically coherent, and therefore superior, system of ideas of which it is not itself a part. Ideas of imagination or confused experience, which constitute our common-sense knowledge, are incomplete in the sense that they do not represent the true order of causes in Nature; they cannot in any case wholly represent the order of causes in Nature, since their *ideata* are human bodies which are only finite modes, subordinate parts of Nature. If they did wholly represent the true order of causes in Nature, then they would be ordered and connected in a deductive system; they would in fact constitute the one complete deductive system, 'the infinite idea of God' (*infinita idea Dei*), or 'the absolute infinite intellect'.

Sense-perception therefore provides us neither with complete and coherent knowledge of external bodies nor with complete or coherent knowledge of our own body; for the ideas of confused experience represent only inter-actions between my body and other things; they do not adequately represent the causes of these interactions. As we ascend the scale of levels of knowledge from mere dreaming through veridical perception to scientific knowledge, our ideas of the modifications of our bodies become more and more 'concatenated' or logically coherent, and so we can be said to understand more and more fully the causes of these modifications. Spinoza takes as an example our knowledge of the sun; at the lowest level of knowledge the sun appears to us as about 200 feet from the earth or as a small round disc; this idea, *considered in itself*, is not false, if interpreted at its proper level as an idea of a modification of our body, and if it is so far left unrelated to any other ideas of modifications of our body. At the next level of knowledge this idea is replaced as false and inadequate by another idea of the sun as a very large object millions of miles away, where this idea is part of that more comprehensive set of ideas which constitutes our common-sense conception of the sun; the first idea is then seen to be inadequate in a larger context of ideas, although adequate at its own level. As we ascend from the common-sense level to the scientific level of ideas or judgements, our ideas progressively reveal more of the causes of the modifications of our body, in the sense that the ideas of these modifications are parts of the whole system of logically related ideas which constitute the science of astronomy. If we were to advance to the highest level of knowledge, the system of ideas or judgements which constitutes the science of astronomy would be absorbed and replaced by a larger system, which would be the single, all-inclusive system of logically concatenated ideas; astronomy would be merged in a unified science, and we would understand intuitively why our particular perceptions of the sun must be as they are.

At the lowest level of knowledge and experience, ideas of imagination are associated in such a way that the presence of one idea suggests another. This passive association of ideas is to be distinguished from the logical concatenation of ideas which constitutes genuine thinking; the order in which ideas of the imagination become associated is not an order of logical necessity, and for this reason must be said to constitute a passivity rather than an activity of the mind. Following Descartes, Spinoza even attempts a physiological account of the association of ideas of sense and imagination in terms of traces in the physical brain. Whatever may be the physical equivalent of remembering and entertaining images, we find in our experience certain characteristic 'linkages of ideas' which are 'not in accordance with the order of the intellect', but which are 'in accordance with the order and linkage of the affections of the human body' (*Ethics Pt.* II. *Prop.* XVIII. *Note*). All our ordinary common-sense and pre-scientific knowledge is constituted by such non-logical associations of ideas; we have accepted most of the propositions which constitute our so-called knowledge on the basis of testimony, habit, and memory, and not as the result of any systematic and logical investigation; most of our ideas or judgements have lodged themselves in our passive minds as the effect of repetitions in the modifications of the body.

At this point, probably influenced by Hobbes and partially anticipating Hume, Spinoza gives an account of ordinary empirical belief and of common-sense knowledge which is sometimes neglected by commentators attracted by his rationalist metaphysics. In his philosophy as a whole, and particularly in his moral theory, his affinities with Hobbes are almost as important as his affinities with Descartes; this emerges very clearly in his account of the formation of the general ideas which are the elements of our ordinary thought and language. These general ideas and concepts form themselves as a result of the incapacity of the body, and therefore of the mind which is its idea, to be modified or affected in more than a limited number of ways. Each modification of the body, the mental aspect of which is a perception, leaves some physical trace, and these traces, superimposed on each other, coalesce into some composite trace; their coalescence is reflected in the mind as a composite image, which is a general idea or 'universal notion' (*notio universalis*). I form the general notion of 'man' or 'humanity' as a result of my body having been affected many times in such a way that I have had many ideas of particular men; these particular ideas have as a result coalesced into a blurred notion of 'man' in general. The common notion so formed is no more than a confused, composite image; it is of the nature of the human body that every impingement or affection of it, disturbing its equilibrium, leaves some trace; therefore it is of the nature of the human mind that every idea of the imagination is stored in the mind, ready to be revived. Consequently in the common order of our experience certain stock ideas automatically build themselves into our mental life; but these ideas are no more than confused images or 'imaginations' (*imaginationes*), and are not clear and distinct ideas arising from explicit definitions and deliberate logical analysis. It follows that the common notions of ordinary discourse, and all ideas of the imagination, are subjective, in the sense that two persons will have the same or similar ideas and general notions only in so far as they have had the same or similar experiences – that is, in so far as their bodies, and therefore their minds, have undergone the same modifications. The relations between ideas in ordinary experience below the level of scientific knowledge are personal, and are in this sense casual and arbitrary. We normally learn the words of a language by means of this purely passive and arbitrary association of ideas; we do not learn to use them, as we learn to use the language of mathematics, by attending to definitions and by deliberately tracing logical connections. Words themselves enter our experience as no more than written marks or sounds, which are so far simply ideas of modifications of the body; they become signs by becoming associated with other ideas of modifications of the body, so that the idea which is the word calls up another idea; and this other idea in its turn is an image of something to which the word is used to refer. We are able to communicate successfully enough for practical purposes in so far as we have roughly similar experiences, and, in so far as we occupy similar positions in the modal system of extension, and therefore in the modal system of thought. All human bodies are of roughly the same structure, and react in similar ways to similar external influences; the formation of their ideas must be correspondingly similar. Even the passive reception of ideas of imagination, which constitutes the ordinary mental life of the majority of mankind, is thought (*cogitatio*) in Spinoza's sense of this word; he uses the word as a generic term to include every kind of mental life, and does not confine it to the activity of the intellect; perceiving, entertaining images, feeling emotions or having internal sensations, no less than thinking and judging, must be modifications of Nature conceived under the attribute of thought; for perceiving, entertaining images, feeling an emotion or having a sensation, are all cases of having an idea which is an idea of some bodily modification; and any idea must have its place in Nature as conceived under the attribute of thought. But such ideas reflect only the transitory affections of a finite mode of Nature, and do not reflect the order of causes in Nature as a whole.

But our passive, unreflecting, common-sense experience and knowledge provide the means of transition to the higher level of genuine scientific knowledge. In addition to the ideas of the imagination, some 'adequate' ideas must necessarily be formed as our mind continuously reflects the modifications of the body in the course of ordinary experience; and genuine scientific knowledge (*Ratio*), which is knowledge of the second kind or level (*cognitio secundi generis*), by definition consists of 'adequate' ideas. As all bodies are modes of Extension, and all minds are ideas of these modes of extension, the universal and all-pervasive features of extended Nature must be reflected in our ideas; although many of the ideas which constitute our minds reflect only the particular modifications of a particular finite mode, some at least must reflect the universal properties of Extension already discussed. Spinoza explains how we each possess the elements of adequate knowledge: 'These things which are common to everything, and which are equally in the part and in the whole, cannot be conceived except in an adequate manner. Hence it follows that some ideas or notions exist which are common to all men; for all bodies agree in some things, and those things are bound to be conceived by all in an adequate manner, that is, clearly and distinctly. There will then exist in the human mind an adequate idea of properties which are common to the human body and any external bodies by which the human body is generally affected, and are present equally in the parts and in the whole of them' (*Ethics Pt.* II. *Prop.* XXXVII, *Coroll.* and *Prop.* XXXIX). These ideas which are common to all men Spinoza calls 'common notions' (*notiones communes*); the 'common notions' must be carefully distinguished from the 'universal notions'. These common notions are the foundations, or starting-points, of our genuine reasoning (*ratiocinii nostri fundamenta*) and of scientific knowledge (*fundamenta rationis*). The objects of such ideas, their *ideata*, are those properties which any mode of extension or any body, or any part of one, necessarily possesses merely in virtue of being a mode of Extension. What distinguishes common notions from universal notions is that the former impose themselves as logically necessary to the conception of extended things as such, while the universal notions are constituted by a confused mixture of logically unrelated ideas. Evident examples of common notions are our ideas of Extension itself, of motion, of solidity, and the whole range of ideas which, in logical reasoning and analysis, can be deduced from these foundations. Spinoza himself could not have conceived his philosophy, or claim to have made himself understood, without appealing to these common notions. Mathematics in general, and geometry in particular, is the science which Spinoza had chiefly in mind as entirely founded on common notions; the fundamental notions and propositions of geometry and arithmetic impose themselves as self-evidently defining the universal and necessary properties of things. As soon as even a single one of such common notions presents itself, the gateway to systematic knowledge is open; from the analysis of any one of such notions the system of properties which constitutes Nature as Extension can be deduced.

A common notion is an 'adequate' idea, clearly and distinctly conceived; it is the mark of an adequate idea that, as soon as presented, it conveys certainty; for it represents something which, in the logically necessary constitution of the universe, could not be otherwise. Therefore it provides in itself a standard of certainty and self-evidence by comparison with which all other ideas and judgements can be assessed as claims to genuine knowledge. Since we all, in the course of common experience, necessarily acquire such common notions and adequate ideas, we must all possess a standard by which we can discriminate genuine knowledge from the confused and uncertain judgements of uncritical common-sense. This doctrine – that all men necessarily know the distinction between logically necessary propositions, which are certainly true, and propositions which can logically be conceived to be false – is fundamental in Spinoza's philosophy. Upon this doctrine he rests his claim that a study of philosophy, which includes the theory of knowledge, is essential to morality and happiness, and his claim that philosophy, which teaches us the right direction of the understanding, has a practical and moral function. He intended his *Treatise on the Correction of the Under-*

standing to be a practical guide to the right use of the mind, in the same sense in which a treatise on health, which he thought equally necessary, would be a guide to the right use of the body. The whole programme of purifying the mind of confused and inadequate ideas depends for its possibility, not only on everyone necessarily having adequate ideas or clear and distinct conceptions, but also on their being able to recognize them as adequate. Spinoza insists that, in order to develop a *method* of right reasoning, it must be taken for granted that, when we have genuine knowledge, we necessarily realize that we have genuine knowledge; to acquire and apply the method must be to have ideas of ideas, and so to have what he calls 'reflexive knowledge' (*cognitio reflexiva*). When, as philosophers, we investigate and classify our own knowledge into its different grades, we must in this process be having ideas of ideas, second-order ideas. These second-order ideas bear to the first-order ideas the same relation as these latter bear to extended things – namely, that for every idea there necessarily exists an idea of this idea, as for every extended thing there necessarily exists an idea of this extended thing; therefore, provided that we have one adequate idea, we *eo ipso* have a method to guide us in distinguishing adequate from inadequate ideas.

To study the method of right reasoning is not itself to get to know the causes of things. It yields that knowledge whereby we know what knowledge is. The method explains what a 'true idea' is, by distinguishing it from all our other perceptions and by investigating its distinguishing marks. By studying the method of right reasoning, we may come to know our own power of clear thinking, and may learn to discipline our minds so that we shall make a true idea the norm in all our thinking. 'The mind, by acquiring an ever-increasing stock of clear ideas or knowledge, *eo ipso* acquires fresh "instruments" to facilitate its progress. For it results from what has been said that there must exist in us, first of all and before everything else, a true idea – the innate instrument, as it were, of our intellectual advance; and that the first part of the method consists in reflecting upon this initial true idea, in forming a true idea of it . . .' (*On the Correction of the Understanding, Section* VII, *para* 39). Spinoza is here again stating his logical position in opposition to Descartes, or rather as a correction of Descartes'. Descartes had prescribed his famous method of clear and distinct ideas as an infallible method of scientific discovery; but, following the necessity which Spinoza is here making explicit, Descartes needed first to be able to indicate at least one clear and distinct idea or self-evident proposition, which could be taken as the 'ideal or norm' of a self-evident proposition; and he thought that he had found such an ideal in the proposition *Cogito, ergo sum;* the Cartesian method of clear and distinct ideas must be founded on this prior example of the *Cogito;* therefore acceptance of the proposition *Cogito, ergo sum,* cannot without circularity be justified solely by reference to the method, that is, on the ground that the proposition *Cogito, ergo sum* is clearly and distinctly conceived. Descartes must choose: either acceptance of the proposition *Cogito, ergo sum* is justified by reference to the method of accepting only clear and distinct ideas, or this method itself is justified by reference to the *cogito*, which is independently accepted as the standard of a true proposition. Descartes' method of clear and distinct ideas might be, and sometimes has been, interpreted as though it were a method of discovery, a new method of acquiring knowledge which is secure and indubitable; but, as Spinoza suggests, it cannot be more than an explicit recognition or formulation of a method already, and independently, in use. Descartes, unlike Spinoza, does not stress this distinction – which has become fundamental in modern logic – between first-order knowledge and second-order or reflexive knowledge; in fact he tries to evade it; he sometimes writes as if the method *is* the reasoning by which we get to know the causes of things, whereas it must be the *statement* of the reasoning by which we get to know the causes of things, that is, 'reflexive knowledge'. Descartes' own procedure in fact exhibits this truth, although he does not clearly acknowledge it by drawing Spinoza's distinction between ideas or judgements of the second-order, which presuppose ideas or judgements of the first-order as their objects. Having admitted one judgement (the *cogito*) as self-evidently constituting indubitable knowledge without prior reference to a justifying method, and as being itself the paradigm on which the method is based, Descartes had in effect conceded the distinction without admitting it.

'Truth is the criterion of itself and of the false, as light reveals itself and darkness.' 'He who has a true idea, knows at the same time that he has a true idea, nor can he doubt concerning the truth of the thing.' 'Truth is its own standard' (*Ethics Pt*. II. *Prop*. XLIII and *Note*). In having a true idea, which, in Spinoza's use, is the same as to entertain a self-evident or necessary proposition, I cannot (as Descartes suggested that I could) doubt its truth; I cannot doubt simply because it is a proposition which is self-evident and logically necessary. If I have knowledge which is genuine knowledge, in the sense that the contradictory of what I know is logically inconceivable, I necessarily know that I know. Descartes' method of doubt, if applied to logically necessary propositions, is a logical impossibility; and only logically necessary propositions can be accepted as constituting certain knowledge. Spinoza argues that, if I can be said to doubt that which is logically indubitable, then I must admit to total scepticism, and must for ever deny the possibility of any certain knowledge; for I cannot then appeal to any idea or judgement as self-justifying; and to seek further justifications or foundations of knowledge must be to pursue assurance down an infinite regress. Therefore I must take my stand at the first step, knowing that an adequate idea, clearly and distinctly conceived, cannot be denied or doubted. Logical necessity or self-evidence is its own guarantee, and no better guarantee can in principle be found.

At this point the argument leads inevitably to what is the central tenet of his logic – namely, to a qualified form of what is called the coherence theory of truth. The coherence theory of truth has had a famous subsequent history, and was most explicitly formulated by the British idealist philosophers who followed Hegel; among the British idealists H. H. Joachim, the foremost English expositor of Spinoza, made an extreme form of the theory explicit in his book *The Nature of Truth*. But, apart from the particular philosophical schools with which explicit formulations of the theory are associated, it recurs as an implicit assumption, unacknowledged and in different disguises, in all phases of philosophy; and it is always associated, as in Spinoza, with doctrines of degrees of truth and reality, and with an *a priori* discrimination of different levels of knowledge. A case might even be made for saying that it is *the* central logical doctrine on which almost all deductive metaphysics or *a priori* 'theories' of the Universe are based; it can be argued that, without some form of this logical doctrine being assumed or accepted, no such philosophical 'explanations' or 'theories' would be attempted. It is therefore worth careful investigation, even apart from its place in Spinoza's system. And within Spinoza's system it is essential, in the sense that he could not have maintained his main metaphysical premise – the Universe as one substance revealed to us in the two attributes of Thought and Extension – without at the same time maintaining some form of the coherence theory of truth. Whether the logical doctrine led to the metaphysical, or the metaphysical to the logical, is a matter of disputed interpretation, as it is in the parallel case of Leibniz's logic and metaphysics; but such disputes are usually unprofitable, since philosophical positions are not generally inferred from a single, fixed premise, but present themselves to their authors as wholes, however at first ill-defined; as a matter of psychological fact, this seems to be the natural way of philosophical discovery or invention, whatever may be the later order of exposition. What is not disputable is that a peculiar form of the coherence theory of truth is a logically necessary part of Spinoza's system, and of any metaphysical monism or One-Substance doctrine.

An 'adequate idea' is defined as 'an idea which contains in itself all the intrinsic marks or properties of a true idea, so far, as it is considered in itself without relation to its object (*Ethics Pt.* II. *Def.* IV); and the explanation attached to this definition is: 'I say intrinsic, in order to exclude that mark which is extrinsic, namely, the agreement (*convenientia*) between the idea and its object (*ideatum*).' An adequate idea reflects the essence or real nature or defining properties of its object or *ideatum:* in another terminology, a self-evident proposition states a logically necessary connexion between the properties of a thing. Merely by attending to such a proposition and its 'intrinsic' content, I can decide that it is adequate; it bears the marks of self-evident truth on the face of it, and no comparison with an external reality is required. A real definition which states the essential properties of extended Nature is the example which Spinoza gives of an adequate idea; in so far as I perceive that logically necessary connexion between the properties which is stated as necessary in the definition, then I know that the definition is adequate and true. In the case of simple thoughts (*cogitationes*) or judgements, the criteria of adequacy and truth necessarily coincide; I can do no more than attend to the logical certainty conveyed. The problem of method in constructing systematic knowledge, and of avoiding error and uncertainty in the construction, is to find by analysis the simple ideas from which the whole order of adequate ideas can be deduced; it is essentially a problem of discovering the order of adequate ideas and of arranging my ideas in what Spinoza calls 'the order of the intellect' (*ordo intellectus*). If I can find among my adequate ideas some simple ideas from which the remainder can be deduced, then I immediately know, as a matter of logical necessity, that this system or concatenation of ideas is the true system; for I know that there cannot be two systems of ideas which are complete and comprehensive. To try to entertain the possibility of two entirely consistent systems of ideas is to try to suppose something which is self-contradictory; it is equivalent to supposing that there might be two self-causing and self-maintaining substances, and it is for the same reasons impossible. Any doubt which I may have about the truth or adequacy of a set of ideas or propositions entails a doubt as to whether this set of propositions can be exhibited as part of a complete and unitary deductive system. The degree of adequacy and truth of ideas must depend ultimately on the degree of comprehensiveness of the logical system of which they can be shown to be a part. An absolutely true and adequate idea of the single comprehensive system is revealed only in 'intuitive knowledge' (*scientia intuitiva*) of the highest

level; and all knowledge must be judged as an approximation to this intuitive grasp of a single system of ideas
reflecting the Universe as a whole. The philosopher
who possessed intuitive knowledge, would understand
immediately, and without need of argument, his own
situation, and that of all the particular things around him,
as necessary parts of the whole structure of Nature.

At this point again Spinoza's logic can be most easily
understood as a criticism of Descartes; the criticism again
takes the form of pushing to a logical conclusion what is
implicit in Descartes' conception of true knowledge as
consisting of clear and distinct ideas. Descartes allowed the
possibility that a system of clear and distinct ideas, that is,
of logically necessary propositions, might not be true, in
the sense that the ideas might not correspond to reality; he
allowed that it is logically possible, in the absence of any
proof to the contrary, that God is a deceiver, in the sense
that propositions which commend themselves as self-
evident and indubitable in the natural light of reason may
not necessarily correspond to external reality. Some proof
is needed to establish that God cannot be a deceiver and
that we are not the victims of a malicious demon; with the
aid of such a metaphysical proof, and only with its aid, it
can be shown that 'the order of the intellect' must reflect
the order of Nature. At least one existential proposition –
either the existence of myself or the existence of God or
both – has to be accepted as true independently of all else, in
order to establish a bridge connecting my clear and distinct
ideas with existing things. The logical counterpart of

Descartes' metaphysical dualism of Thought and Extension is that a logical sequence of ideas cannot be immediately and necessarily assumed to reflect the order of causes in Nature; a further guarantee is required that ideas which are clear and distinct are also true, in the natural sense of corresponding to reality. It is this dualism which seemed to Spinoza untenable in the last analysis, no less as a logical than as a metaphysical doctrine; he argued that, unless we accept the self-evidence of a proposition as not only a necessary, but also a sufficient, condition of its truth, we must be led into total scepticism by way of an infinite regress; for any argument designed to establish that a logically indubitable proposition must be accepted as true must itself presuppose what it is designed to establish. This is the force of the aphorism 'Truth is the criterion of itself' (*Ethics Pt.* II. *Prop.* XLIII. *Note*); for if it is once allowed that a proposition which is self-evident and logically necessary may not be true, any argument to remove this sceptical doubt must presuppose what it is trying to prove, and so be circular. Thus Spinoza's logic, no less than his metaphysics, develops naturally out of the apparent inconsistencies of Descartes; and just this necessary connexion of truth with logical adequacy is required by the metaphysical monism which represents Thought and Extension as two attributes of the unique substance; for to speak of Thought and Extension as two attributes of a single substance is to allow no doubt of *correspondence* between thought and the external world; idea and *ideatum* cannot in any case fall apart.

Following from, or connected with, this account of truth

as an intrinsic property of ideas or propositions, falsity and
error have a characteristically different interpretation in
Spinoza and Descartes. For Spinoza error, and what is
ordinarily called having a false belief, can never be absolute, but must always be a matter of having relatively
incomplete knowledge; one can be said to have a false
belief in so far as one has knowledge (in the generic sense)
only of the lowest level – that is, in so far as one has an
idea derived from mere sense perception, memory or
imagination. But there is no sense in which any belief or
idea can be said to be false absolutely and without qualification; for even an idea, which we would normally describe
as a mere fiction or vagary of the imagination, has its own
ideatum and is necessarily the reflexion of some modification of a finite mode in Nature. It is rightly dismissed as a
vagary of the imagination when it can be shown to exhibit
the causes of things even more inadequately than our other
ideas – that is, to be even less consistent with the fragmentary system of our ideas than is normal. It is in this sense
that Spinoza insists that error is always the privation of
knowledge; to say that an idea or proposition is false is to
say that it is relatively incomplete or fragmentary, and is
therefore to say something about its lack of logical relation
to other ideas; the falsity is corrected as soon as the idea is
placed in connexion with other ideas in a larger system of
knowledge. Secondly, error or false belief cannot, as
Descartes had maintained, arise from an infirmity of the
will in assenting to, or deciding to accept as true, an idea
which is not clear and distinct in the light of reason;

according to Spinoza there can be no mental act of assenting, which, when confronted with an idea or proposition, we are in any sense free to perform or not to perform. The human mind cannot be, within Spinoza's metaphysics, a free agent, or an agent of any kind, in affirming or denying; for an individual mind simply consists of ideas of the modifications of that finite mode which is my body; and these ideas occur in an order which is determined within the order of Nature as a whole. We are victims of delusions of the imagination and of other forms of error in so far as our mind consists of the confused perceptions of the senses and of memory, and of the mere passive association of ideas; in so far as our mind consists of clear and distinct ideas deduced from 'common notions', our ideas *cannot* be confused; false belief and superstition are at this level impossible, since, by definition, false ideas cannot co-exist in my mind with genuine scientific knowledge, that is, with ideas which reflect the order of causes in Nature. I *cannot* conceive the sun as a small round disc, or accept such a description of it as a true and adequate description, if I have adequate knowledge of the causes of this confused idea – that is, if I understand the causes of the particular modification of my body of which this idea is the reflexion.

At this point we encounter for the first time the central crux of Spinoza's philosophy and of any such systematic metaphysics – namely, the paradoxes of the complete determinism which is involved. The kind of knowledge which my mind possesses is necessarily linked with the power or disposition of my body to be affected to a

greater or less extent by changes in extended Nature
(*Ethics Pt.* II. *Prop.* XIV and *Dem.*); my mental ability
and my physical ability are substantially the same ability
conceived under two different attributes; modifications of
my mind are always and necessarily the counterpart of
modifications of my body, and the modifications of my
body are the counterpart of the modifications of my mind.
What distinguishes a person from the lower animals and from
so-called inanimate objects is that a person is a more complicated organism liable to be affected by its environment
in a greater variety of ways; it is therefore able to reflect
more of the order of causes in Nature as a whole. A person
could permanently have absolutely complete knowledge –
knowledge of the highest grade (*scientia intuitiva*) – if, and
only if, his body reflected the order of causes in extended
Nature as a whole; but in the limiting case in which the
ideas constituting a person's mind are the counterpart of
the whole order of causes in extended Nature, that 'person'
would be not a person or finite mode, but (actually
identical with) God or Nature; only if his body had
become identical with Nature conceived as Extension could
his mind permanently possess absolutely complete knowledge. In so far as his knowledge approaches this perfection,
it follows logically that his body must correspondingly
become disposed to be affected in a greater variety of ways;
given Spinoza's account of the mind-body relation, which
is itself inseparable from the conception of Thought and
Extension as two attributes of the single substance, there
can in principle be no intellectual progress without a

corresponding extension of what we would distinguish as the physical powers of the organism. The implication of ordinary language is that I may, by an effort of will and attention, expand my scientific knowledge or philosophical understanding without my physical condition changing; but this seems to be excluded by Spinoza's terminology. In fact our ordinary language is fundamentally Cartesian, at least in the sense that it allows us to conceive of the powers of the mind as *logically* independent of the powers of the body, however constantly they may *in fact* be found to be causally connected. But for Spinoza the human organism is a finite mode which cannot properly be conceived as consisting of two causally interacting substances or quasi-substances, but must be conceived to change or be modified as a whole; he dismisses the common-sense representation of the human mind and the human body as two quasi-substantial entities as no more than a confused imaginative picture, which dissolves under analysis.

It may seem difficult to understand how Spinoza can allow that, by the deliberate adoption of a purely intellectual method and discipline, the understanding can be corrected or amended, or how the study of the theory of knowledge, providing ideas of ideas (*cognitio reflexiva*), can have any practical effect or usefulness. It would seem that each of us has the knowledge which he has because of the particular subordinate position which he occupies in the scheme of Nature, and that by no mere effort of will can our relative ignorance be remedied. Yet there can be no doubt that the *Treatise on the Correction of the Understanding* was intended as a *practical* guide to salvation: its famous introduction says – 'Before all things, a method must be thought out of healing the understanding and purifying it at the beginning, that it may with the greatest success understand things correctly. From this everyone will be able to see that I wish to direct all sciences in one direction or to one end, namely, to attain the greatest possible human perfection' (*Correction of the Understanding Pt.* II). The theory of knowledge is introduced as a necessary means to salvation, where salvation involves a state of complete and permanent well-being. The theory of knowledge is represented in this respect as parallel, and complementary, to medicine and to the theory of the education of the young; all three are essential as providing practical methods of self-improvement. The conception of logic as teaching the art of thinking and so teaching the way to true and certain knowledge, and *therefore* teaching the way to salvation and happiness, is the classical conception which descends from Plato; in the seventeenth-century logic of Port Royal and Descartes, it was still largely taken for granted that to learn logic is to learn to think clearly and correctly. But Spinoza's own account of logic and theory of knowledge as providing second-order knowledge, *cognitio reflexiva* or ideas of ideas, suggests the contrary view – that in philosophical reflexion we become aware of the nature of our own ideas or knowledge, but not that we thereby acquire the means to change them or to 'correct the understanding' at will. If our second-order ideas are the reflexion in idea of first-order ideas or knowledge, and these are the reflections in idea of the modifications of the body, how can our ideas be changed, or our understanding corrected, by the deliberate application of any logical method? To talk of applying a method suggests that it is a matter of will or decision to arrange our ideas in accordance with a chosen pattern or order, as Descartes had required; but Spinoza had allowed no sense to will or assent in this context; the human mind is not an ultimately free subject or substance which can affirm or deny at will. In the Preface to the Fifth Part of the *Ethics* (*On the Power of the Intellect or Human Freedom*) Spinoza does in part meet this point in discriminating his position from Descartes'. He observes that because Descartes had represented mind and body as interacting, the point of interaction being what he called the pineal gland, he could represent the will as directing the attention of the bodily senses; at least in this respect a person may be said to acquire knowledge or ideas deliberately or at will; and therefore for Descartes it is logically possible for a person to choose to apply a logical method, and to set himself deliberately to acquire knowledge in accordance with it. But, Spinoza argues, this direction of the mind by the will can only be allowed to be intelligible at the cost of admitting the union of body and mind, as two substances or quasi-substances, to be altogether unintelligible; as soon as Descartes' conception of the union of mind and body is admitted to be unintelligible, voluntary control either of the understanding or of the passions becomes questionable.

The whole question of human freedom, and of our powers of voluntary self-improvement, will be discussed in the next chapter. What is here important is that the possibility of any individual attaining that highest grade of knowledge, which is essential to complete happiness, rests on the inclusion among his ideas of those common notions on which all science and organized knowledge are built; this at least is guaranteed to him, since his body is a finite mode of Extension, and as such must present to his mind those intuitively self-evident propositions which reflect the essential features common to all modes of Extended substance. We all have flashes of perfect knowledge, and therefore have glimpses of what *scientia intuitiva* would be. Secondly, every individual possesses in these self-evident or logically indubitable propositions a standard or norm of necessary truth and genuine knowledge; these exemplary truths provide everyone with the means of discriminating 'vague experience' and irrational and subjective opinion from genuine knowledge; we do not need to be taught what genuine knowledge is, because we all necessarily possess some specimens of it among our ideas, and, in possessing them, necessarily recognize them for what they are; the marks of objective truth and logical certainty are intrinsic; the logician or epistemologist, in distinguishing the different levels of knowledge, merely draws attention to distinctions which we have already implicitly recognized. So much as this seems indisputably Spinoza's doctrine. The difficulties of interpretation begin when we adopt the standpoint of the individual seeking inprovement and consider the different levels of knowledge and of under-standing which different individuals may have attained; then we will ask ourselves whether, by the freely chosen and deliberate adoption of a logical method or by voluntary practice of the art of thinking, we can as individuals freely decide to improve ourselves, and by this resolution escape from error and superstition. The nearest to a definite answer to be found in Spinoza comes in *Letter* XXXVII. Having there explained that in the concatenation of clear and distinct ideas the mind is free from external causes, and is able to distinguish between the work of the Intellect and the work of the Imagination, he remarks in conclusion: 'It remains however to warn you that for all these (pur-poses) there are required assiduous reflexion (*assiduam meditationem*) and a most constant mind and purpose. To gain these, it is first of all necessary to decide on (*statuere*) a definite mode and plan of life, and to set before one a definite end' (*Letter* XXXVII). This passage, taken by itself, suggests that Spinoza's answer is the Cartesian and common-sense one – we can improve our understanding by deliberately choosing and adhering to a way of life and a discipline; it is a matter of making the necessary effort. But if we turn back to the *Ethics* to find what is required in order to impose on ourselves a plan of assiduous meditation, we find that the possession of scientific knowledge is an indispensable condition for making such a choice; and so we seem to go round in a circle which cannot be broken into at any point by a mere act of will; only the 'native strength' of the mind in understanding can help us.

In studying logic or the theory of knowledge, we become self-conscious and explain to ourselves the imbecility of our reason and the relative inadequacy of our knowledge; we explicitly recognize that most of our so-called knowledge does not reflect the true order of causes in the Universe, but is only a logically confused association of ideas, reflecting our individual reactions to our limited environment. We explicitly formulate to ourselves 'the way' to true and certain knowledge, a way which we have always more or less clearly known; even the least philosophic or scientific men, at the lowest level of understanding, are able to distinguish the relatively true from the relatively false; they must accept those propositions which are more logically coherent in preference to those which are less so, even in making their common-sense judgements about the world. They have not reflected, as philosophers and logicians, on their own procedure in distinguishing truth from error at their own level, and have not held in view as the ultimate standard, as the Spinozist does, the ideal of perfect knowledge; they are unreflectively satisfied with half-truths and confused imaginations; but they are so unphilosophically satisfied with their own level of imperfect knowledge, because they are no more than finite modes within Nature. So it seems that the amount of progress which any individual person makes, or can make, along that way is definitely limited and is to be explained by his particular situation as a particular finite mode.

Spinoza's logic and theory of knowledge, which is logically inseparable from his metaphysics, is designed as the necessary introduction to his moral teaching; the title of his work, 'Ethics,' is just and essential. Although he (perhaps) cannot argue that, in studying his theory of knowledge, we are provided with the means of choosing the right way to live as free men, we are at least provided thereby with *the means of distinguishing* between freedom and servitude. His metaphysics and dependent theory of knowledge are designed to show man's place in nature as a thinking being, Spinoza always arguing that, until this is understood, nothing can be said about the nature and possibility of human happiness and freedom. Ethics without metaphysics must be nonsense; we must first know what our potentialities are and what our situation is as parts of Nature; otherwise anything we say about human purposes and happiness must be relatively subjective; our statements will be no more than a projection of the desires and imaginations generated in us by our particular confined experience as finite modes in Nature. Only in so far as we somehow come to understand ourselves and our actual and possible purposes *sub specie aeternitatis*, that is, as necessary consequences of our situation within *Natura Naturata*, can we lay down moral propositions which are objectively valid.

But, before passing from Spinoza's theory of knowledge to ethics in the strict sense, his theory of knowledge must first be characterized and assessed for its own sake, partly because commentators are so apt to stress one of its diverse elements at the expense of others, and partly because it exhibits in the most uncompromising form a doctrine or method which is constantly recuring in philosophy. His philosophy, and particularly his theory of knowledge, is liable not to be appreciated as a whole, although itself severely consistent, because it is linked simultaneously to two normally divergent and opposed tendencies and traditions – the extreme nominalist tradition of Hobbes and the high idealist and rationalist tradition associated with the coherence theory of truth. He is a nominalist in his doctrine that all the general terms and classificatory concepts of our ordinary language represent only the confused, composite images generated in each one of us by the particular order of his own sense-experiences. All our ordinary beliefs or statements expressed in terms of qualitative distinctions – e.g., about the colours of objects or about our own desires and feelings – are subjective, and cannot be taken as expressions of genuine knowledge. Consequently all inquiries into the essences of particular things or of natural kinds, all classificatory science and all the disputes of the schoolmen, are illusory; the whole of traditional Aristotelian logic, requiring a plurality of substances classifiable by *genera* and species, must be discarded; and all metaphysical disputes, involving such transcendental notions as Being, are from the beginning senseless. A quasi-physiological explanation can be given of the formation of universal notions, which are no more than confused images arising out of the repetition and association of particular images. So far Spinoza's logic (see particularly *Ethics Pt.* II. *Prop.* XL. *Notes* I and II) is of the pattern to be found in Hobbes and many subsequent empiricist philosophers. Nominalism of this extreme form has generally in the history of philosophy been the introduction to a radically sceptical position which denies the possibility of all metaphysics and of any logically certain knowledge of the world – as in Hobbes himself, in Hartley, James Mill, Bain and in many others of a continuous line. But in Spinoza it is used to lead to the opposite conclusion; we are able to recognize the inadequacy of our common-sense knowledge and our ordinary classifications only because we possess a norm or standard of genuine knowledge with which to contrast them. This norm or standard is provided by the logically indubitable propositions of mathematics, the terms of which are not confused images formed as a result of sensory experience, but clear and distinct conceptions, formed by the active intellect. By quoting specimens of mathematical truisms to illustrate what he means by the higher grades of genuine knowledge, Spinoza returns to the tradition which descends ultimately from Plato through Descartes; this traditional argument, if pursued with absolute consistency, must always lead (I shall now argue) to some form of the coherence theory of truth and to the monistic metaphysics, which Spinoza in fact associates with it.

The skeleton of the rationalist argument is: as soon as we begin to reflect on and criticize our claims to knowledge with a view to improving them, we first distinguish between what we know with certainty and beyond all possibility of doubt or error, and what we claim to know only with the accompanying possibility of error; the problem of logic, which teaches the art of thinking or of correcting the understanding, is to find a method of eliminating the possibility of error. As soon as the demand for a logical method which eliminates the *possibility* of error is accepted as a demand which can be satisfied, one is already committed to rejecting as valid claims to knowledge all propositions which cannot be *proved* to be true, in the mathematical and strictly logical sense of 'proof'; for to say 'I have a method to show that this cannot be false' seems the same as to say 'I can prove this'. But, even more important, as soon as we ask for a *method* of distinguishing true propositions from false propositions, in order to eliminate the *possibility* of error, we are in effect asking for a *criterion* by which true propositions can be distinguished from false. A method is essentially something which can be stated in general terms and applied in particular cases; in order to remove the possibility of error, we must be able to state what conditions must be satisfied before a proposition can be accepted as true, and then carefully examine any proposition presented to determine whether it satisfies these conditions. Any such *general* criterion or *general* method for distinguishing truth from error would enable us to decide whether a particular proposition is true *without considering its particular content;* in any general proposal for distinguishing true from false propositions, discovering whether a proposition is true is identified with discriminating some intrinsic, logical properties of the proposition concerned, irrespective of its particular content; and this identification, which follows directly from requiring a *general* method of eliminating the *possibility* of error, is precisely what is involved in the coherence theory of truth. To discover whether a particular proposition can safely be accepted as true must always be to discover something about the logical properties and relations of the proposition, as opposed to discovering something about the world; it is to do logic, as opposed to observing things and events. Therefore what is ordinarily called empirical knowledge, or knowledge of matters of fact, as distinguished from the recognition of logical necessities, is already excluded from any claim to consideration as genuine and certain knowledge; for to formulate a general method or criterion must be to formulate a logical method or criterion, and a method of eliminating the possibility of error must be a method of eliminating purely factual or empirical statements; for by definition a factual statement is a statement in respect of which error is always in principle possible, in this sense of 'possible'. Merely to undertake such a search for infallible knowledge, and to admit that the demand for it makes sense, is in itself implicitly to accept Spinoza's definition of genuine knowledge as necessarily expressed in a set of necessary propositions, or as being a logical concatenation of clear and distinct ideas; for to talk in this context of general methods of eliminating error, and of criteria of truth, is always to suppose some substitute in the acquisition of knowledge for the fallible comparison of particular propositions with the facts of observation and experience. An empiricist would argue that it cannot make sense to ask under what conditions *any* proposition may be accepted as certainly true, or to look for a *general* method of distinguishing truth from error; he would try to show that this question can only be significantly asked and answered of *particular specified* propositions or propositions of a specified form or on a specified topic; for in each and any case, deciding on the truth of any factual or informative proposition must involve attending to its specific content; and this in itself must preclude the possibility of any general or logical method of eliminating error. But this is precisely to deny that truth 'guarantees itself', and to deny that we can take the clarity and distinctness of an idea (its adequacy) as the necessary and sufficient guarantee of its truth; and this is to deny the whole basis of Spinoza's logic.

To attack the basis of his logic at this point is also to attack the basis of his metaphysics; for his metaphysics is a consistently sustained denial of the possibility of comparing ideas with some independent and external reality, with which our ideas may or may not correspond.

This is why the theory of truth has been central in modern empiricism; metaphysical systems seem so often to have arisen from the self-defeating question – 'Under what conditions is a proposition (= any proposition whatever) true?': there *can* be only one answer – 'It depends on the proposition'; but to have shown this was (strangely) a great achievement of modern logic.

CHAPTER FOUR

Freedom and Morality

MAN is part of Nature, and therefore the moralist must be a naturalist; no moral philosopher has stated this principle of method more clearly, or adhered to it more ruthlessly, than Spinoza. The actual servitude and unhappiness of man, and his ideally possible freedom and happiness, are both to be impartially deduced and explained as the necessary consequences of his status as a finite mode in Nature; exhortation and appeals to emotion and desire are as useless and as irrelevant in moral as in natural philosophy. We must first understand the causes of our passions; our whole duty and wisdom is to understand fully our own position in Nature and the causes of our imperfections, and, by understanding, to free ourselves from them; man's greatest happiness and peace of mind (*acquiescentia animi*) comes only from this full philosophical understanding of himself.

Human beings are finite modes within Nature, which, like all other particular things, persist and retain their identity only so long as a certain total distribution of motion and rest is preserved among the system of ultimate particles (*corpora simplicissima*) composing them; they constantly suffer changes of state or modifications of their nature in interactions with their environment; but, being relatively complex organisms, they can be changed in a great variety of different ways without their cohesion, or their 'actual essence' as particular things, being destroyed. The identity of any particular thing in Nature logically depends on its power of self-maintenance, that is, on its power to maintain a sufficiently constant distribution of energy in the system as a whole in spite of constant changes of its parts; the 'actual essence' of any particular thing simply is this tendency to self-maintenance which, in spite of external causes, makes it the particular thing that it is. This is part of the meaning of the all-important *Proposition VII* of *Part* III of the *Ethics*: 'The endeavour (*conatus*) wherewith each thing endeavours to persist in its own being is nothing more than the actual essence of the thing itself.' The greater the power of self-maintenance of the particular thing in the face of external causes, the greater reality it has, and the more clearly it can be distinguished as having a definite nature and individuality. Within Spinoza's definitions, therefore, it is necessarily true that every finite thing, including a human being, endeavours to preserve itself and to increase its power of self-maintenance; the *conatus* is a necessary feature of everything in Nature, because this tendency to self-maintenance is involved in the definition of what is to be a distinct and identifiable thing.

This point needs to be emphasized to avoid misunderstanding of Spinoza's moral theory. That all men seek first their own preservation and security appears in Hobbes and in many other philosophers as a supposed truism on which moral and political philosophy must be founded. Whatever may have been Hobbes' intention, the army of philosophers, psychologists and economists who have followed him in accepting this premise have generally accepted it simply as a fact about human nature, and as confirmed by dispassionate observation of human conduct. Other philosophers and psychologists, opposing Hobbes, have simply denied that it is confirmed by observation; they have argued that, as a matter of fact, it is untrue. This controversy about human psychology, whatever its merits, is largely irrelevant to Spinoza's moral theory; he also says that all men seek first their own preservation and the extension of their own power; but, in saying this, he is not simply making a statement about the observed facts of human behaviour; he is deducing a consequence of his own account of individuality, a consequence which is applicable, not peculiarly to human beings, but to all finite things. Therefore, in order to refute his contention, it is neither necessary nor sufficient to cite propositions of empirical psychology; it is necessary to show that in general his whole terminology is either inapplicable or inconsistent, and to attack the logical system of which this doctrine is a part.

Human beings maintain their identity or individuality for a limited period of time by maintaining a more or less constant adjustment of their parts; this self-maintenance is not the outcome of choice or decision, but occurs naturally and necessarily to all things in Nature. Other particular things, which are less complex in their structure than persons, are susceptible of fewer modifications and have less individuality as distinct things; their cohesion is liable to disruption by a comparatively narrower range of external causes. All things and their modifications can be conceived as parts of Nature either under the attribute of Thought or under the attribute of Extension. Human beings are of that degree of complexity which we describe, when conceiving them under the attribute of Thought, by saying that they are self-conscious, or that they have minds; animals, being less complex in structure as extended or physical things, are correspondingly not complex enough, conceived as animated or thinking things, to be described as self-conscious or as having minds. A human mind consists of ideas which reflect the effects of external causes in modifying that balance of motion and rest which constitutes a human body. A modification, arising out of a body's interaction with other things, may be either an increase or a diminution of vitality or energy; and vitality or energy may vary within comparatively wide limits without the personality being destroyed. These changes of state, which can be described in physical terms as rises and falls in the vitality of the organism, can be described in mental terms as pleasure and pain; every increase in vitality or energy is by definition a pleasure, and every depression of vitality is necessarily a pain. Spinoza is not stating – as a modern psychologist might – that there is a *correlation* between an increase in physical vitality, defined in terms of some physical tests, and the felt sensation of pleasure; he simply *means* by the word 'pleasure' (*Laetitia*) 'the passion by which the mind passes to a higher state of perfection, and by pain (*Tristitia*) the passion by which it passes to a lower state of perfection' (*Ethics Pt.* III. *Prop.* XI. *Note*). Any increase in the power or perfection of the body must be an increase in the power or perfection of the mind and conversely; an increase or decrease in vitality can always be conceived indifferently in either mental or physical terms.

The degree of power or perfection of any finite thing depends on the degree to which it is causally active, and not passive, in relation to things other than itself. The one absolutely powerful and perfect being, God or Nature, is in all respects active and in no respects passive; for God is self-determining, and none of his modifications can be the effects of external causes, since there can be no causes external to God or Nature. A finite mode, such as a human being, has a greater power and perfection in so far as its successive states or modifications are less the effects of external causes and are more the effects of preceding changes within itself. Thus a human being, conceived as a finite mode of Thought, has greater power or perfection in so far as the succession of ideas which constitute his mind are linked together as causes to effects; he is active and not passive, in so far as the succession of ideas is a logical one (for Spinoza does not, and cannot, distinguish between the 'cause of an idea' and the 'logical ground' of an idea); he has less power or perfection as a thinking being in so far as this autonomous process of thought is interrupted by ideas which are the effects of external causes on him, and in so far as his present ideas are not explicable as the logical consequences of previous ideas in his mind. In an absolutely powerful and perfect thinking being, there would simply be an infinite sequence of ideas each one of which would be logically related to its predecessor – God as a thinking substance being the '*Infinita Idea Dei.*' Most human minds consist of a comparatively random sequence of ideas, random, not in the sense that they are not the effects of causes of some kind, but in the sense that the causes are external to the sequence; the sequence is therefore not in itself intelligible as a self-contained sequence. The power and perfection of an individual mind is increased in proportion as it becomes less passive and more active and self-contained in the production of ideas. Spinoza is less explicit about what constitutes an increase in the power or perfection of a human being conceived as a particular extended thing or body; he does not clearly explain what is the equivalent in physical terms of the transition from the illogical association of ideas to logically coherent thought. He must (I think), in view of his own premises, have left it to be inferred that the equivalent in physical terms of free intellectual activity is that internal stability of the organism, which enables it to persist without any violent fluctuations produced by external causes; the mind is relatively free and active in its thinking when the body is relatively in a constant state in relation to its environment, and is freely functioning without great exchanges of energy. But, in the absence of his projected treatise on the outlines of a science of medicine, this interpretation must remain speculative.

Human beings can be said to be aware of the tendency to self-preservation and to the increase of their own power and activity which constitutes their 'actual essence' as individuals; the reflexion in idea of this *conatus*, which is common to all particular things in Nature, is called desire (*cupiditas*). Desire is defined as appetite (*appetitus*) together with consciousness of it; appetite is the *conatus*, or tendency to self-preservation, expressed neutrally, that is, neither in purely mental nor in purely physical terms. Similarly the transition to a state of greater power or perfection in any individual is reflected in his consciousness as pleasure, and a diminution of power as pain. It is important in Spinoza's moral philosophy that pleasure and pain always represent a *change* in psycho-physical state; they are the mental reflexion of the rise or fall in the power or activity of the organism. Such a change may be produced, in any particular case, by any variety of external causes; what particular things will promote or depress the vitality of any particular individual depends on the constantly changing nature of that individual; it depends on the particular state of the individual organism, that is, on the particular configuration of its ultimate elements at the moment of its interaction with the external cause. It is therefore meaningless to speak of any external things as absolutely, or in themselves, pleasant or painful. Although there may be some things which in fact are always or generally sources of pain or pleasure to most human beings, we cannot discover them by *a priori* reasoning, or by considering the intrinsic properties of the things themselves; we must study the sources of pleasure and pain scientifically in relation to the changing states of organisms. Within these definitions, desire and pleasure are interpreted – and, given Spinoza's ultimate premises, must be interpreted – as natural states or modifications of the person, which occur independently of will or judgement: or rather, will and judgement about what is pleasant or desirable are defined in terms of, and allowed no meaning apart from, the natural and necessary tendency of the human organism to maintain and increase its own power and perfection; its power and perfection I shall summarily call its vitality. The crucial passage is the *Note* to *Prop.* II of *Part* III of the *Ethics*, from which I will quote only a few sentences ... 'The mind and the body are one and the same thing, which is conceived now under the attribute of thought, now under the attribute of extension. From which it comes about that the order of concatenation of things is a single order, whether Nature is conceived under one or the other attribute; it follows therefore that the order of the actions and passions of our body is simultaneous in nature with the order of the actions and passions of the mind ... Now all these things clearly show that the decision (*decretum*) of the mind, together with the appetite and determination of the body, are simultaneous in nature, or rather that they are one and the same thing, which, when it is considered under the attribute of thought and explained in terms of it, we call decision, and when considered under the attribute of extension, and deduced from the laws of motion and rest, we call determination (*determinatio*) . . .' Any individual at any moment of his existence is, regarded as a body, in a condition to be stimulated or depressed in vitality by contact with certain things; this condition or 'determination' is completely explicable by purely physical laws and in terms of physical equilibrium and of the recent disturbances of this equilibrium. The same situation can equally well be described by saying that the person desires or will enjoy certain things, or that he judges these things to be good or desirable; to say that he has freely decided to pursue these things, or that he judges them to be good, is not to describe something which is separable from his 'determination' or physical condition; it is merely to describe the condition in another terminology, or to conceive the modification under the attribute of thought rather than of extension. The popular terminology of 'will' and 'judgement' is unscientific, or represents confused perceptions, because it does not represent the causes of a person's condition; indeed the suggestion of the words 'will' and 'judgement', as they are ordinarily used, is that there are no such causes and that will and judgement are free and undetermined; and this is nonsensical.

In the remainder of this important *Note* Spinoza uses an argument against objectors which, like so many of his arguments, is a remarkable anticipation of arguments which are current, and seem convincingly new, to-day; it is the kind of anticipation which justifies one in regarding his system and his definitions as in many respects more relevant to present interests than Descartes'. He has to meet the objection that we cannot plausibly suppose that such higher activities of persons as, for instance, the design of buildings and the painting of pictures, can be exhibited as the effects of purely physical causes, or as being in principle deducible from some laws governing the energy of particles; in describing the more elaborate human plans and purposes, it seems that we must always recognize an irreducible and substantial distinction between the higher activities of the mind and the more simple functioning of the body, even if we may in fact discover some causal relations between them. This is the objection. Spinoza's answer to this old, and still popular, argument is: 'No one has so far determined what the body is capable of, that is, no one has yet been taught by experience what the body is capable of doing merely from the laws of Nature alone, in so far as Nature is considered as purely physical nature, and what it cannot do, unless determined by the mind. For no one has acquired such accurate knowledge of the fabric of the body, as to be able to explain all its functions; nor need I omit to mention the many things observed in brutes, which far surpass human sagacity, and the many things which sleep-walkers do, which they would not dare to do when awake: this is sufficient to show that the body itself, merely from the laws of its own nature alone, can do many things, at which the mind marvels' (*Ethics Pt.* III. *Prop.* II. *Note*). Spinoza is here arguing that we are not justified in excluding *a priori* the *possibility* of physical explanation of any part of human behaviour; for such an exclusion can only be based on an argument from ignorance; the difference between the lower mental activities, of which we are ready to admit a corresponding description in physical terms, and the higher activities, is merely a difference of degree of complication. We are already prepared, and perhaps even compelled, to admit that relatively elaborate patterns of behaviour – e.g. the behaviour of animals and of sleep-walkers – can be explained in physical terms, without any appeal to faculties of will or judgement; even in our ordinary, common-sense terminology, behaviour may be in most observable respects indistinguishable from so-called purposive behaviour without being called purposive in any sense which excludes physical explanation. Once this is admitted, there remains no *a priori* justification for drawing a line, and for excluding the possibility of description and explanation in physical terms, at any particular point on the scale of complication; we may in our common-sense descriptions fall back on the terminology of will and purpose, simply because purely physical explanations and descriptions are not yet in fact available; the use of these words 'will' and 'purpose' confesses that we do not in fact generally possess clear and adequate ideas of causes; they are confessions of ignorance, which philosophers, conspicuously Descartes, have erected into metaphysical dogmas grounded on logical principle. The strength and originality of this argument is the recognition, both as against Descartes and as against seventeenth-century materialists such as Hobbes and Gassendi, of the possible, but still unimagined, complication of physical structures and physical laws. It is the importance of so stressing the almost unlimited complexities of physical structures which most clearly emerges in all recent discussions of the relations of mind and body against the background of twentieth-century scientific knowledge. Descartes, and the rationalists and materialists of his own age (and even up to the present day), conceivèd matter or the extended world as essentially simple in structure, and as governed in its motions by essentially simple geometrical principles, or by essentially simple mechanical laws. The paradigm of a physical system was a piece of clockwork; only that part of human behaviour which could be described and explained by the use of concepts which are also applicable to clockwork could be regarded as explicable in physical terms; in so far as human behaviour cannot be assimilated to the behaviour of clockwork, no explanation which is clear and intelligible can be looked for; the prevailing assumption was that only more or less simple mechanical systems – and the physiologist must exhibit the human body as such a system – can be regarded as intelligible physical systems. Thus the dichotomy – a person as a machine regulated by causal laws or a person as a free and causally inexplicable spiritual substance – persisted long after Descartes; throughout the two following centuries a materialist was someone who tried to show that human thought and behaviour can be analysed into more or less simple mechanical patterns. In the last fifty years, physicists have abandoned the more simple mechanical models as essential to all physical explanation, and have admitted vast complexities of structure of an unmechanical kind, not only in the study of the human brain, but in other branches of biology and physiology; Spinoza's argument has again become important. Any scientist or philosopher must to-day be prepared to admit that 'no one has yet been taught by experience what the body is capable of doing merely from the laws of Nature alone, in so far as Nature is considered as purely physical' (*Ethics Pt.* III. *Prop.* II. *Note*). This must be left an open question; and there can be no *logical*, but only empirical, grounds for closing it; and certainly no general conclusions can be based on our present ignorance of the powers and structure of the human brain and body.

Spinoza's theory of *conatus*, of desire and will, is designed to show the full implications of admitting the possibility of complete causal explanation of human behaviour. He has so defined these basic terms that it follows logically that all men pursue their own pleasure in accordance with the necessary laws of Nature; they necessarily pursue pleasure, not in the sense that they always in fact deliberate about what will give them most pleasure and then choose to act accordingly, but in the sense that their so-called choices, and their pleasures, can always be explained as arising from the *conatus* of the organism, its tendency to self-maintenance and self-preservation. Anything of any kind may accidentally be a source of pleasure or of increased vitality, or of pain and of decreased vitality; the reaction depends on the psycho-physical condition of the organism at a particular time. In so far as the idea of a particular external cause comes to be associated in my mind with a sense of pleasure or increased vitality, I can be said to love the thing taken to be the external cause, and I will consider the thing good; whatever comes to be associated in my mind with pain or a sense of depressed vitality, I can be said to hate and will consider bad. The succession of ideas which constitutes my mind is, as explained in the last chapter, normally governed by laws of association; one idea calls up another because they have occurred together in the past, or because similar ideas have occurred together in the past. By the agency of these laws of association in the imagination, the whole complex system of our desires and aversions is formed. Whatever becomes associated in our mind with something which is associated with pleasure, itself becomes an object of desire; and this association of ideas may proceed to any degree of complication. Thus objects which, considered in themselves, are not the direct or primary causes of pleasure or pain in me, may indirectly become associated with pleasure or pain.

Pleasure, pain and desire are taken by Spinoza as the primary passions in terms of which all the other passions or emotions are to be defined. They are passions, not only in the popular sense of the word, but also in his technical sense; in ordinary life (special conditions will be described later) they arise, as described, from the *passive* association of ideas; in so far as they arise from the passive association of ideas, they are by definition 'confused' perceptions, in which the mind is not aware of the causes of its ideas. In experiencing these passions, we are merely reacting to

external causes; our conscious life is proceeding at the level
of sense-perception and imagination, and not at the level
of logical thought or active intellect. When in ordinary life
we enjoy and pursue, hate and avoid various kinds of
things, the ideas constituting our minds are 'inadequate',
and the judgements we make about these things unscientific; for these ideas or judgements exhibit only the interactions between our bodies and other parts of nature, and
do not show the true causes of the modifications of our
body; the ideas accompanying these modifications of the
body 'indicate the actual constitution of our own body
rather than that of the external bodies' (*Ethics Pt.* II.
Prop. XVI. *Coroll.* II); but they exhibit neither the nature
of our own bodies nor of external bodies adequately,
in their proper place in the order of causes in nature.
These are the grounds of Spinoza's famous distinction
between active and passive emotion, the first of his contri-
butions to the theory of conduct; the distinction derives
directly from the epistemological distinction between
imagination (inadequate ideas) and intellect (true and
adequate ideas). There is nothing in Spinoza's vocabulary
which exactly corresponds to the ordinary distinction
between 'feeling an emotion' and 'thinking'; as his doctrine
is that every modification of the body involves at the same
time having an idea, every kind and phase of consciousness
involves having an idea, including even the mere experiencing of an emotion. The word *affectus*, although it comes
the nearest to the word 'emotion' in the familiar sense,
represents the whole modification of the person, mental

and physical. The 'affection' is a passion (in Spinoza's technical sense) in so far as the cause of the modification or 'affection' does not lie within myself, and it is an 'action' or active emotion in so far as the cause does lie within myself; this is another way of saying that any 'affection', of which the mental equivalent is not an adequate idea, must be a passive emotion; for an adequate idea is an idea which follows necessarily from the idea which preceded it. I am active in so far as I am thinking logically, that is, in so far as the succession of ideas constituting my mind is a self-contained and self-generating series; I am passive, in so far as my succession of ideas can only be explained in terms of ideas which are not members of the series constituting my mind; for in this latter case the ideas constituting my mind must be, at least in part, the effects of external causes. My ordinary hates and loves, desires and aversions, succeed each other without any internal logical connexion between the ideas annexed to them.

This argument is at first difficult to grasp because we do not now use the word 'cause' as Spinoza and other philosophers of his time used it; it is strange to us to identify *the cause* of a certain idea in my mind with the *logical ground* from which this idea can be deduced; but the distinction between active and passive emotions, and indeed the whole of Spinoza's moral theory, depends upon this identification. To re-state: I experience an active emotion, if and only if the idea which is the psychical accompaniment of the 'affection' is logically deducible from the previous idea constituting my mind; only if it is so deducible, can I be said to have an adequate idea of the cause of my emotion. If the idea annexed to the emotion is not deducible from a previous idea in my mind, it follows that the emotion or 'affection' must be the effect of an external cause, and that I am in this sense passive in respect of it. As the ideas constituting my mind are the psychical equivalents of the modifications of my body, I can only have adequate knowledge of the causes of those of my 'affections' which are not the effects of external causes. If the cause of the 'affection' is external to me, it follows that it involves an inadequate idea, and the converse must also be true; therefore, to say that the cause of the modification is external to me is *equivalent* to saying that it involves incomplete knowledge and an inadequate idea. In so far as I am a free agent, unaffected by external causes, I necessarily have adequate or scientific knowledge, and the converse must also be true; only the intelligent man can (logically) be free, and only the free man can (logically) be intelligent. But human beings, as finite modes, cannot in principle be *completely* free and unaffected by external causes; human freedom must be a matter of degree. Spinoza's method in the last three parts of the *Ethics* is to contrast the actual and normal conditions of human servitude with the humanly unattainable ideal of permanent and perfect freedom.

In his survey of the normal conditions of our emotional life, Spinoza attempts to define the ordinarily recognized emotions in terms of his primary 'affections' – pleasure, pain and desire. There had been several previous attempts to systematize the vocabulary of the emotions; and such systems of definitions were generally conceived as explanations of the 'essence' or 'true nature' of the various emotions. But in Spinoza's design, the names of the emotions – jealousy, anger, fear, envy and so on – are not in themselves taken to be important, nor are his definitions primarily intended to enlighten us as to the 'true nature' of each particular emotion named in the common vocabulary. It is one of the first principles of his logic, throughout nominalistic, that definitions of the abstract, general terms of ordinary language cannot yield genuine knowledge; it is nonsense to talk of the essence of jealousy common to your jealousy and to mine. He strongly insists (*Ethics Pt.* III. *Prop.* LV. *Note* I) that the joy of one man is essentially different from the joy of another, although the common name is properly applicable to them both; the difference between the two experiences depends on the particular nature ('actual essence') of the particular individuals involved, and this in turn depends on their particular situations in Nature. To understand the two experiences is to situate each of them in the chain of causes in Nature as a whole; it is useless to inquire into the vague similarities which the common abstract name represents. The catalogue of the emotions, and Spinoza's analyses of them in terms of pleasure, pain and desire, serve mainly to show that the emotions can be understood and interpreted on his principles, and as ultimately arising from the *conatus*, the tendency to self-preservation, which is common to all things in Nature, human or inhuman; secondly, the catalogue serves to exhibit in convincing detail the varieties of human servitude and unreason. The emotions which we ordinarily distinguish – ambition, lust, pity, pride, anger, and many others – are shown to be differentiated only by the way in which the primary passions of pleasure, pain and desire are evoked. In our ordinary experience of this whole range of emotions, we are 'agitated by contrary winds like waves of the sea, waver and are unconscious of our issue and our fate' (*Ethics Pt.* III. *Prop.* LIX. *Note*); this is one of the very few uses of rhetorical metaphor in Spinoza's writing; to him, as to Montaigne, man in his normal condition is essentially *chose ondoyante*, pathetically unstable and unreasonable. The list of the emotions at the end of Part III of the *Ethics*, although mainly intended to illustrate the manifold complications of desire and its objects, contains many acute psychological observations, for example, on the natural alternation between love and hatred of the same person. Spinoza, in his detached and impersonal style, notices the twists and perversities of human feeling and behaviour more closely than most of the philosopher-psychologists of his age; he is conspicuously less schematic and crude than Hobbes, and is nearer to the great French moralists in his calm pessimism. The many philosophers who have tried to show the varieties of human feeling and behaviour as deducible from a primary urge towards pleasure and self-preservation have generally over-simplified the intricacies of human behaviour; they have made men appear more starkly rational and self-seeking than they are. Spinoza was not in this sense rationalistic, and allows for the literally infinite varieties of human folly and help-lessness literally infinite, because the pleasures and pains of each individual are essentially different, depending on his individual constitution and his position in Nature. In emphasizing the helpless irrationality of normal human loves and hates, desires and aversions, and their independence of conscious thought and purpose, Spinoza is once again nearer to modern psychology than to the commonplace psychology of his contemporaries; he is certainly less shallow than Descartes, who seemed uninterested in the less conscious sources of human weakness; he rejects the facile optimism of Descartes' appeals to will and reason. In order to understand the reactions of an ordinary man, we must attend, not to his own statements about his feelings and motives, but, first, to his particular physical constitution and, secondly, to the trains of unconscious association and habit which have been established by his particular experiences. An unenlightened man's own accounts of his motives and behaviour will be what we now call rationalizations; he will give plausible reasons for feeling and behaving in certain ways, but these reasons, expressed in terms of deliberate choices and decisions, will not give the true causes of his reactions. The ordinary man in his rationalizations will speak as if his desires and aversions were determined by the properties of external objects; if he really is an ordinary and not a philosophical man, he will not see his desires and aversions as determined by his own constitution and past experience, until these causes are pointed out to him.

The transition from the normal life of passive emotion and confused ideas to the free man's life of active emotion and adequate ideas must be achieved, if at all, by a method in some respects not unlike the methods of modern psychology; the cure, or method of salvation, consists in making the patient more self-conscious, and in making him perceive the more or less unconscious struggle within himself to preserve his own internal adjustment and balance; he must be brought to realize that it is this continuous struggle which expresses itself in his pleasures and pains, desires and aversions. Hatred and love, jealousy and pride, and the other emotions which he feels, can be shown to him as the compensations necessary to restore loss of 'psychical energy'. There is an evident parallel between Freud's conception of *libido* and Spinoza's *conatus*; the importance of the parallel, which is rather more than superficial, is that both philosophers conceive emotional life as based on a universal unconscious drive or tendency to self-preservation; both maintain that any frustration of this drive must manifest itself in our conscious life as some painful disturbance. Every person is held to dispose of a certain quantity of psychical energy, a counterpart (for Spinoza at least) of his physical energy, and conscious pleasures and pains are the counterparts of the relatively uninhabited expression and frustration of this energy. Consequently, for Spinoza no less than for Freud, moral praise and blame of the objects of our particular desires, and of the sources of our pleasure, are irrelevant superstitions; we can free ourselves only by an understanding of the true causes of our desires, which must then change their direction. According to both Freud and Spinoza, it is the first error of conventional moralists to find moral and *a priori* reasons for repressing our natural energy, our *libido* or *conatus;* they both condemn puritanism and asceticism in strikingly similar tones and for roughly similar reasons. Asceticism is only one expression among others of the depression of vitality and the frustration of the *libido* or *conatus;* however we may deceive ourselves, our feelings and behaviour, even what we distinguish as self-denial, can always be explained as the effects of drives which are independent of our conscious will. Consequently both Spinoza and Freud represent moral problems as essentially clinical problems, which can only be confused by the use of epithets of praise and blame, and by emotional attitudes of approval and disapproval. There can in principle be only one way of achieving sanity and happiness; the way is to come to understand the causes of our own states of mind. Vice, if the word is to be given a meaning, is that diseased state of the organism, in which neither mind nor body functions freely and efficiently. Vice, in this sense, always betrays itself to the agent as that depression of vitality which is pain; vice and pain are necessarily connected, as are virtue and pleasure; this is another way of saying that, in Spinoza's sense of the word, 'virtue is its own reward'. Pleasure, in this primary sense of the felt tone of efficiency of the organism, is distinguished by Spinoza from mere local stimulation, which he calls 'titillation' (*titillatio*). When we ordinarily speak of pleasure or pleasures, we are referring only to these temporary and partial stimulations; and because of this use of the word it appears paradoxical to assert a necessary connexion between virtue and pleasure; but in this contest pleasure (*laetitia*) is contrasted, as the organism's sense of entire well-being, with pleasure in the more common sense of a temporary excitement. This contrast between a sense of total well-being and a mere temporary stimulation has a long philosophical history from Plato onwards; perhaps it corresponds to something in our experience which is reflected in the ordinary association of the words 'happiness' (*laetitia*) and 'pleasure' (*titillatio*). But I suspect that all such precise labelling and classifying is irrelevant for anyone who would really explore the varieties of human experience.

Other points of comparison could profitably be found between the two great Jewish thinkers, Freud and Spinoza, each so isolated, austere and uncompromising in his own original ways of thought. The points of detailed resemblance between them follow from their common central conception of the *libido* or *conatus*, the natural drive for self-preservation and the extension of power and energy, as being the clue to the understanding of all forms of personal life. Neither crudely suggested that all men consciously pursue their own pleasure or deliberately seek to extend their own power; but both insisted that people must be studied scientifically, as organisms within Nature, and that only by such study could men be enabled to understand the causes of their own infirmity. Consequently both have been attacked for insisting on an entirely objective and clinical study of human feeling and behaviour. Lastly, there is a similarity, evident but more difficult to make precise, in the grave, prophetic, scrupulously objective tone of voice in which they quietly undermine all the established prejudices of popular and religious morality: there is the same quietly ruthless insistence that we must look in every case for the natural causes of human unhappiness, as we would look for the causes of the imperfections of any other natural object; moral problems cannot be solved by appeals to emotion and prejudice, which are always the symptoms of ignorance. They have both provoked the hatred which visits anyone who would regard man as a natural object and not as a supernatural agent, and who is concerned impassively to understand the nature of human imbecility, rather than to condemn it. In reading Spinoza it must not be forgotten that he was before all things concerned to point the way to human freedom through understanding and natural knowledge.

FREEDOM AND MORAL STANDARDS

Our normal life is a series of agitations and 'fluctuations' of the mind reflecting the manifold influences to which we are subject in the unceasing modifications of Nature; we feel pains, pleasures, and desires, and experience a flow of complicated and ambivalent emotions. We naturally associate these agitations, in our confused ideas, with external persons and objects as their causes. Spinoza points out that we are trained and conditioned as children to hate some things and to love others, and to associate the ideas of some things with pain and of others with pleasure. By habit and association we come to call some things good and other things bad; we call things good, in one common use of the word, if the idea of them, as a result of something in our past experience, causes us pleasure, and if they have become, consciously or unconsciously, objects of desire. As human beings are generally similar to some degree in their psycho-physical structure and are generally subjected to roughly similar external influences, there must in fact be some things which most normal men generally desire or enjoy; the things which are generally the objects of normal appetites, or the idea of which is normally associated with pleasure, are called good, in this quasi-objective sense of the word; those things, of which the idea is in fact generally depressing to normally constituted men, are called bad in this sense. Spinoza can allow that the moral epithets 'good' and 'bad' are popularly and intelligibly used in this quasi-objective sense; so far they have the same use as words like 'pleasant' or 'admirable'; they indicate the appetites and repugnances of the user, or what happen to be the tastes of most normal men. But it is important to notice that in this popular use the epithets must not be interpreted as referring to the intrinsic properties of the things or persons called good or bad; they refer rather to the constitution and reactions of the persons applying the epithets. But there is a natural extension of this popular use of the words 'good' and 'bad'. We naturally come to speak of 'normal' men and the 'normal' constitution of man; in talking of 'man' in the abstract, we are led to form a universal notion, or vague composite image, of what a man should be, or of the type or model of a man. We are then inclined to think of this type or ideal of a man as we think of an ideal house or an ideal theatre; objects which are created by human beings with a definite purpose, artifacts such as houses or theatres, can properly be said to conform more or less closely to a norm or ideal of what a house should be; we can judge how far any particular house satisfies the purposes for which houses in general are designed. But we are led into confusion when, having formed an abstract universal notion of a natural kind, we come to think of this universal notion as representing the ideal or perfect specimen of the natural kind; we form in this way a general notion of what a man should be, as we form a general notion of what a house should be; and we think of men, as of houses, as more or less perfect in so far as they conform to the ideal. The misleading implication in this way of thinking is that human beings, and other natural kinds, are designed with a purpose. To say of a house that it is imperfect in some respect is to make a statement to which a definite meaning can be attached by an objective test; the statement is tested by a comparison of the actual house with what was projected in the design of it. To say of a man that he is imperfect in some respect looks as if it were to make a statement which is testable by the same procedure, and which looks as if it had a similarly definite sense; but this is wholly misleading, since we must not suppose that human beings, or any other natural objects, have been designed for any purpose; consequently it makes no sense to think of them as fulfilling, or failing to fulfil, a purpose or design. In thinking of particular men as in some respect perfect or imperfect, or as (in this sense) good or bad specimens of their kind, we can only be comparing them with some abstract general notion, which has formed itself in our minds, of what a man should be; and this general notion has no objective significance, but arises only out of our own particular associations; it can be no more than an arbitrary projection of our own tastes, interests and experience. Whenever we hear natural objects discussed as though they were artifacts, we have the most sure evidence of theological superstition; Spinoza will not allow any mention of design or of final causes in the study of Nature.

Spinoza's destructive analysis of the basis of ordinary moral judgements, and of the standards that they imply, follows directly from the basic propositions of his logic. (1) The properties of everything within Nature are deducible from the necessary laws of self-development of Nature as a whole; if something appears to us imperfect or bad, in the sense of 'not what it should be', this is only a reflexion of our ignorance of these necessary laws. If we understood the necessary principles on which the individual nature of particular things depends, we would thereby understand the part that various things play in the whole system. Philosophically speaking, all finite things within Nature are imperfect, simply in the sense that they are finite things within Nature, which alone is complete and perfect; but they all fit perfectly into the system, and could not possibly be other than they are. (2) All general, classificatory terms, distinguishing different natural kinds, are confused images, formed as the effect of an arbitrary association of ideas, and do not represent the real essences of things. To understand the nature of anything is to fit it into the system of causes and effects of which it is a part; all qualitative classifications are subjective and arbitrary. (3) To think of things or persons as fulfilling, or failing to fulfil, a purpose or design is to imply the existence of a creator distinct from his creation; this is a demonstrably meaningless conception. Repudiating the whole traditional logic of classification, and with it the Aristotelian search for the real essences of natural kinds, Spinoza must repudiate the conception of final causes, which was an integral part of this traditional logic. Such phrases as 'the essential nature of man' and 'the purpose of human existence' are phrases that survive in popular philosophy and language only as the ghosts of Aristotelianism, and that can have no place in a scientific language. Popular and traditional morality is largely founded on such surviving pre-scientific and confused ideas. In ordinary moral praise and condemnation, we necessarily imply a reference to some standard or ideal of what a person should be, or assume some end, purpose or design in human existence.

Considered scientifically and in the light of systematic knowledge, nothing can be said to be in itself morally good or bad, morally perfect or imperfect; everything is what it is as the consequence of necessary laws; to say that someone is morally bad is, in popular usage, to imply that he could have been better; this implication is always and necessarily false, and is always a reflexion of incomplete knowledge. Spinoza can allow no sense in which 'good' and 'bad' can be applied to persons which is not also a sense in which the words are applicable to any other natural objects, whether brutes or things. It is this disturbing contention which is the core of the metaphysical issue between determinism and free-will, and this issue we must now consider.

The phrases '*morally* good' and '*morally* bad' and their equivalents have generally been used, at least in Europe, in such a way as implicitly to distinguish human beings from animals and inanimate objects. It is part of the force of the word 'moral' that only human beings can significantly be judged as morally good or bad, because only human beings can be said to deliberate and to choose; what distinguishes human beings, as the possible subjects of *moral* judgements, is that in general it makes sense (although it is often false) to say of a human being that he could have acted in some different way if he had chosen. It was Spinoza's 'hideous hypothesis', and the only part of his philosophy which immediately became generally famous, that this criterion of distinguishing human beings as exercising rational will and choice is mere superstition; it is a superstition which must be rejected as we advance up the scale of natural knowledge. He did not deny, and no philosophical determinist could plausibly deny, that, as language is ordinarily used, we do in fact speak of persons, as opposed to animals and inanimate objects, as being free to choose between alternative courses of action. But his determinism cannot be refuted by the type of argument which philosophers to-day are apt to use in attacking such metaphysical theses – namely, by an appeal to such standard uses of language; for he is criticizing, and giving reasons for criticizing, the ordinary uses of language as superstitious, and as reflexions of inadequate ideas and pre-scientific thinking. He is maintaining that we will necessarily abandon the notion of freedom of choice as our knowledge and understanding of Nature, and of human nature as part of Nature, increase; and this is a more formidable thesis. The argument of a metaphysical determinist such as Spinoza seems simple and compelling. As we progressively acquire more and more scientific knowledge of the behaviour and reactions of human beings, more and more of their actions are shown to be deducible from laws of nature; this is a mere tautology, since by 'scientific' knowledge we simply mean the explanation of events as deducible from laws of nature. If a human action is shown to be deducible from a law of nature, that is, is exhibited as the effect of a cause, there is at least one sense in which we must say that the agent could not in this case have acted otherwise, or that no alternative action was possible; and if no alternative action was in this sense possible for him, it seems unreasonable to allow a sense to saying that he could have acted otherwise if he had chosen.

Therefore, as our psychological and physiological knowledge of human actions and reactions increases, the range of human actions of which we can reasonably say 'an alternative action was possible', or 'he could have acted otherwise', necessarily diminishes; this seems to amount to saying that any statement of the kind 'an alternative action was possible', or 'he could have acted otherwise', is necessarily a sign of the incompleteness of our scientific knowledge, or an expression of our present state of ignorance: and this was precisely Spinoza's contention.

He expresses this simple and formidable argument elliptically and in his own terminology, using his basic logical distinction between adequate ideas, which are logically necessary propositions, and inadequate ideas, which are contingent propositions, or propositions which could (logically) be false. In so far as we have adequate knowledge, we understand someone's actions as the necessary effect of a cause; in so far as our ideas are inadequate, the action is represented in our thought as contingent and uncaused. In Spinoza's logic the discovery of the cause of some event is the discovery of the laws by which the occurrence of the event could be adequately explained; these laws themselves will in their turn be shown to follow from some higher-order premises, and the law will gradually be fitted into the single deductive system which is God or Nature conceived under the attribute of thought; as our knowledge grows, every human action becomes one necessary link in the infinite chain of causes. 'Men think themselves free, in so far as they are

conscious of their volitions and desire, and are ignorant of the causes by which they are disposed to will and desire...'
Superstition is by definition ignorance of causes; when we do not know the cause of something, we superstitiously accept some explanation in terms of the purpose or end for which the thing was done; superstition is belief in final causes. At the most primitive level of superstition, we explain the fall of a stone from a roof as the result of God's will to kill someone; but, as our physical knowledge increases, we discard such supernatural explanations of physical events in terms of final causes, and in terms of acts of will, in favour of purely scientific explanations. But in respect of human actions, involving a more complicated structure of causes, we are still generally in a state of primitive ignorance of causes, and we are therefore content to describe most human behaviour in terms of inexplicable acts of will; such popular, pre-scientific accounts of human behaviour are necessarily displaced by explanations in terms of causes as our knowledge increases, and as the confused ideas of the imagination are replaced by adequate ideas of the intellect; such pre-scientific accounts of personality are characteristic of the lower grades of knowledge (*experientia vaga*), and are naturally reflected in the familiar uses of common-sense language; it is the responsibility of the philosopher to show their inadequacy when judged by those standards of genuine knowledge which we all implicitly recognize. But a philosopher must expect to meet bitter sentimental resistance from those whose desires and fears, loves and hates, are tied to the primitive super-

stitions which represent persons as free and uncaused causes. Admittedly passages can be found in the *Ethics* which, when quoted (as they so often are) out of their context, give the impression that Spinoza was denying that there is anything to be found in our experience corresponding to the notions of 'will' or 'choice'. Such a denial would be plainly absurd; but it is certainly not a necessary consequence of his determinist argument; and he did not (I think) intend it. He need not, and (I think) did not, deny that we are in fact often conscious of a state which we describe as 'choosing between alternatives' or 'deciding by an act of will to do what we do not want to do'; we are often in a state of 'fluctuation of mind' (*fluctuatio animi*), and from this state some decision, often with a peculiar sense of effort, finally emerges. His contention is only that, in giving a coherent, rational account of human actions in terms of their causes, 'will' and 'choice', as psychological phenomena, have no special place; they are just one mode of consciousness among others, one set of ideas among others in the sequence which constitutes our mind. Yet, at the common-sense, pre-scientific level, we talk as if conscious acts of will or deliberate choice in themselves constitute adequate *explanations* of human action, because we are conscious of acts of will and choice, but not of their causes. Such pseudo-explanations mention the agents' conscious purposes, but not the ultimate and true causes of his action, and therefore are inadequate as explanations; for they do not exhibit actions as examples of the necessary features of the natural order, but as merely contingent, and as the effects of the 'free' choices of individuals. But individuals, being finite modes within Nature, cannot be 'free', in the sense that their actions are uncaused; they only appear free to the ignorant, as the falling of the stone appears free to the ignorant; the differences in this respect between the person and the stone lie in the comparative complication of the causes, and in the fact that a person may in his thought follow the true intellectual order of causes. The individual person's consciousness of his own needs and strivings (*appetitus*) is reflected in his consciousness as desire (*cupiditas*). But the desire, which is associated with his pursuit of particular ends, is no more than the reflexion in idea of his total state, which itself is determined by a variety of external and internal causes; we can therefore adequately explain his pursuit of particular ends only in terms of these causes, and not *vice versa*.

Determinism, so ruthlessly stated, is no longer widely accepted, as it was by many untheological thinkers in the nineteenth century; an effort of imagination is now required in order to reconstruct the intellectual conditions in which it seemed generally plausible. The simple faith of Laplace in the theoretical possibility of a complete explanation of every state of the universe is now generally represented as logically absurd. Determinism in this extreme form seems plausible only at a time when the possibilities of *complete* scientific explanation are accepted as absolutely *unlimited*. If it is accepted that a *single* form of scientific explanation is, or must be, in principle applicable to every thing or event in the universe, whatever their qualitative differences and however great their complexity, then it will seem reasonable to reject much of the common-sense language which we ordinarily apply to the choices and decisions of human beings; for the apparent implication of this language, as it is ordinarily used, is that forms of explanation which are applicable to the behaviour of animals and physical things are *in principle* inapplicable to the behaviour of human beings; we seem ordinarily to take it for granted that the type of explanation accepted in physics or biology must be, in kind and in principle, radically different from the kinds of explanation which can be given of rational human behaviour. The idioms of personal description in common language are inherited from periods in which a systematic psychology, parallel with the other natural sciences, was not yet envisaged; they seem to descend from the age of magic; this at least is the thought of a scientific optimist. In the heroic, pioneering and confident phase of modern science, extending roughly from Galileo to Einstein, this last surviving barrier is naturally challenged, and the possibility is envisaged of a single language of science, which will be complete and unlimited in its application; and just this programme of removing the barrier between human choices and the motions of the animal and physical world is the thesis of determinism. Such confident visions of a single system or language of science are less prominent to-day, partly because the actual development of the sciences in the last fifty years has not been generally in accordance with the simple pro-gramme originally envisaged; the various sciences have not in fact tended to conform to a single, simple pattern of mechanical explanation and have not in fact shown a single set of intuitively evident mathematical notions to be sufficient for all purposes. Some of the accepted patterns of physical explanation have been called in question as having only a restricted and not a universal application, and new and more complicated types of theory have been adopted for some purposes. Theoreticians of science are no longer inclined to speak so confidently of a single system of natural law in terms of which all natural events might in principle be explained. They are inclined rather to envisage a variety of overlapping systems of different types, each of which is found appropriate to some specific purpose and in some limited contexts. Consequently metaphysical determinism, of which Spinoza was the most uncompromising proponent, no longer seems such an acute issue to philosophers and moralists; early optimism about the construction of a unified and all-embracing language of science has been, at least temporarily, overclouded; and it now seems questionable whether simple and definite causal explanations of human choices and decisions, explanations not substantially different in type from physical explanations, are likely to emerge from the study of psychology; this is at least considered an open question, which it is wise, as a principle of method, to leave open. Certainly we will always try to establish some systematic theory of human behaviour; but one cannot dogmatically forecast what form the theories will take, or to what degree they will conflict with our ordinary pre-scientific descriptions of human conduct.

These, roughly summarized, are the historical factors which explain why Spinoza's form of determinism is now generally rejected. But the arguments cannot be brushed aside merely on the grounds that, as Spinoza stated them, they depend on his metaphysical thesis of the unity of Nature as a causal system; for the kernel of his argument can (I think) still be re-stated so as to be independent of his metaphysical premise. Spinoza as metaphysician asserts that Nature *must* be conceived as a completely intelligible, infinite and self-contained causal system; any other conception of it can be shown to be logically self-contradictory. But a determinist may reject this inference from the logical coherence of Spinoza's definitions to the nature of reality, and yet may still use the argument that *in proportion as* our scientific knowledge, or knowledge of causes, increases, we necessarily abandon the primitive conception of human beings as undetermined in their choices; he may admit that our scientific knowledge may never in fact be complete, or he may even admit that there can be no sense in speaking of complete scientific knowledge. But he might still maintain that we think of human beings as free agents, to be distinguished in this respect from all other things in Nature, only in so far as we are ignorant of the causes of their behaviour, and in so far as our scientific knowledge is incomplete. In support of his thesis he can point to the fact that, as soon as we do come to understand the causes of a particular kind of human behaviour, we do generally cease to regard people as, in the normal sense, morally responsible for the type of behaviour now causally explained; we do in fact cease to apply purely moral epithets to them as responsible agents. When the behaviour now causally explained is what was formerly regarded as morally wicked, we come to regard it as the symptom of a disease, curable, if at all, by the removal of its causes; expressions of moral disapproval come to seem useless and irrelevant. As psychology in its various branches progresses, the sins and wickedness of free agents come to be regarded as the diseases of patients; the line drawn in our common-sense speech and thought between a disease or pathological condition, for which the sufferer is not responsible, and wickedness, which the agent could have avoided, is gradually effaced in one case after another; young criminals are reclassified as juvenile delinquents, whose anti-social behaviour can be cured by the appropriate treatment, but cannot usefully and reasonably be blamed, with the purely moral implications which formerly attached to such blame; the very words – 'anti-social' in place of 'bad', 'delinquent' in place of 'criminal' and so on – show the gradual erosion of the old common-sense attitude, as scientific knowledge advances. At the level of common-sense, a Spinozist may argue, we adjust our moral attitudes haphazardly, regarding people as free agents whenever we happen to be ignorant of the causes of their actions. But the scientist-philosopher, who tries before all things to achieve intellectual consistency in his thinking, cannot be content with the illogicalities of ordinary usage; he can demonstrate to himself that the range of actions which he can regard as avoidable progressively contracts as scientific knowledge advances; and, secondly, that ordinary usage provides no constant and objectively justifiable principle by which he can distinguish avoidable and morally blameworthy actions from other natural events. As a philosopher, he is conscious of our actual present state of relative ignorance, and he can envisage the possibility of an indefinite advance in the understanding of the causes of human behaviour, whether or not in any particular case the causes have in fact been discovered, or are likely soon to be discovered. According to Spinoza, we know *a priori*, and can prove, that human knowledge must at all stages be limited and incomplete; otherwise it would cease to be human knowledge and would become divine knowledge. But equally we know *a priori* what ignorance is and what complete knowledge would be; for we could not otherwise distinguish, as we do, between adequate and inadequate knowledge; we are able to recognize the inadequacy of our present scientific knowledge in respect of human behaviour, and we can envisage the possibility of our knowledge becoming progressively less inadequate; and this is precisely what the philosopher is doing in maintaining the determinist thesis.

Throughout all his writing, whether on political, religious or purely ethical subjects, Spinoza is constantly pleading, in opposition to traditional theology and respectable opinion, for a purely naturalistic and scientific study of all aspects of human thought and behaviour; he is constantly insisting that emotional and moral attitudes, which can only be the reflexions of our subjective desires and fears, must obstruct us in understanding the causes of our unhappiness and folly, and so must obstruct us in the pursuit of wisdom. If we would improve human beings, we must study the natural laws of their behaviour as dispassionately as we would study the behaviour of trees and horses. In the twentieth century this thesis, although not always combined with belief in strict determinism, is very familiar in theory, though still uncommon in practice; in the nineteenth century it earned for Spinoza the admiration of Flaubert and of many others, who in their time more easily foresaw the necessity of a natural history of human religion, and of moral codes and social structures. But in the seventeenth century, which was still throughout Europe predominantly an age of belief in supernatural causes, a purely naturalistic approach to human affairs was terrifying, and to the ordinary dilettante (as Spinoza's correspondence shows) was almost unintelligible. Spinoza, alone of the great figures of that age, seems somehow to have anticipated modern conceptions of the scale of the universe, and of man's relatively infinitesimal place within the vast system; in Descartes and in Leibniz, and in most of the literature of the age, one is still in various ways given the impression of a Universe in which human beings on this earth are the privileged centre around whom everything is arranged, almost, as it were, for their benefit; whatever their professed doctrine, almost everyone still implicitly thought in terms of a man-centred universe, although Pascal also, in some moments of conflict, had this inhuman vision of human beings as not especially significant or distinguished parts of an infinite system, which seems in itself vastly more worthy of respect and attention than any of our transitory interests and adventures. To Spinoza it seemed that men can attain happiness and dignity only by identifying themselves, through their knowledge and understanding, with the whole order of nature, and by submerging their individual interests in this understanding. I suggest – and this is no more than speculative interpretation – that it is this aspect of Spinoza's naturalism, the surviving spirit of Lucretius against a greater background of knowledge, which most shocked and baffled his contemporaries and successors, and which seemed the most 'hideous' feature of 'the hideous hypothesis'.

WISDOM AND THE LIFE OF THE FREE MAN

We can be said to be free in so far as we follow in our thought the true intellectual order of ideas; to have this adequate knowledge of causes necessarily involves a more complete knowledge of Nature as a whole. In so far as we acquire more knowledge of Nature, and therefore of ourselves as parts of Nature, we necessarily cease blindly to desire, love and hate particular things, and we cease to be governed through our passions by the particular things and persons around us; for these loves and hates arise by the association of ideas out of our ignorance of the true causes of our pleasures and pains. The free and wise man therefore feels morally neutral towards the particular things and persons around him, both because he understands why they are what they are and why they cannot be otherwise, and because he no longer ignorantly sees them as the true causes of his own pleasures and pains. The free man's pleasures must be generated spontaneously, as the consciousness of his own unimpeded activity of mind and not as the effects of external causes. The greater the real activity and vitality of his body, the greater the real activity and vitality of his mind; and the converse is also necessarily true. In so far as a person is functioning freely and is uninhibited by external causes, he will necessarily be in a state of pleasure (*laetitia*), since pleasure in this sense is the reflexion of the vitality of the whole person. It follows that the wise and free man will avoid pain and all the so-called virtues of asceticism; his aim will necessarily be '*bene agere ac laetari*' – 'to act well and to rejoice.' Spinoza, so austere in his personality and life, repudiates all the values of self-sacrifice and self-denial and the gloomier, more unnatural Christian attitudes, such as humility, repentance, and remorse; 'there cannot be too much joy: it is always good: but melancholy is always bad' (*Ethics Pt.* IV. *Prop.* XLII). Pain, and the painful emotions (e.g. hatred, envy, fear), are always and necessarily signs of weakness, or of lack of freedom; they are reflexions of some inhibition of vitality by external causes; particular pleasures in the narrow sense (*titillatio*) may be excessive, as upsetting the balance and well-being of the whole organism; but pleasure in the sense of conscious well-being and enjoyed activity is the characteristic of the free or intelligent man's life; to act well is fully to enjoy oneself, and fully to enjoy oneself is to act well. Suffering, guilt, and remorse are morbid symptoms, and virtue is sanity and health. Anything that is an aid to the development of knowledge and intelligence, and is therefore an aid to power and freedom, is necessarily good for the individual, and is to be pursued in the interests of self-preservation; anything which obstructs knowledge is self-destructive, 'bad' in the only quasi-objective sense of the word, as diminishing the freedom and vitality of the individual. Social and political instability and personal rivalries clearly interfere with that independence and detachment which the free man requires for the pursuit of knowledge. The free man has therefore every interest in upholding the necessary conventions of a peaceful society. Spinoza argues, as so many moralists have argued, that in so far as our desires, loves and hates are not directed towards particular things and persons around us, we are not involved in conflicts with other persons; the happiness of the free man, which is the free exercise of his under-standing, is essentially uncompetitive, and requires from others only peacefulness and respect for law and order. The free man, so far from being competitive, has a positive interest in promoting the happiness and intellectual emanci-pation of his neighbours; and this must be part of Spinoza's theoretical justification of his own lifework. In so far as the members of any society are governed by passive emotions, there must necessarily arise conflicts of interest in the society which must threaten the free man and his self-preservation and self-advancement in knowledge. It is therefore the direct interest of the enlightened and the free man to work (as Spinoza himself methodically did work) to emancipate his fellow-citizens from superstition and ignorance and from the blind hatreds which superstitions engender. 'Whatever helps to maintain the common society of men, or whatever brings it about that men live together in peace and agreement, is useful, and, on the other hand, what produces discord in the state, is bad' (*Ethics Pt.* IV. *Prop.* XL). The happy, wise, and free man (and no one can qualify for one of these three titles without qualifying for the others) is incapable of hating his fellow men, and will, like a Christian, repay hatred, rage and contempt with love; but the reason for this secular saintliness is simply a superior prudence. Hatred is in itself disagreeable and bad, and the wise man knows that the reciprocation of hatreds must produce a greater hatred. The true philosopher will be uninfluenced by fear and hope, and unaffected by the superstitious fears and hopes of the anthropomorphic religions, with their futile imaginations of jealous personal Gods allotting rewards and punishments. He will know that 'virtue is its own reward', in the strict sense that the best life is necessarily the happiest life; the intrinsic satisfactions of the free mind are the most lasting and secure. As free men, we do not need to be bribed, by the hope of rewards or the fear of punishments, like children; no external sanction is needed in addition to the supreme inner satisfaction which arises from a rational peace of mind. Spinoza writes with disgust and contempt of the appeal of conventional religious

morality to supernatural rewards and punishments, as
being appeals which are essentially squalid and unworthy
of adult intelligence. He had, of course, been criticized,
as most secular and humane moralists have been, on the
grounds that, by denying the possibility of a personal
God acting as moral umpire and prize-giver, he was
undermining morality and opening the way to chaos and
debauch. In his contemptuous letters of reply he allowed
himself to be less unimpassioned than anywhere else in
his extant writings.

'A free man thinks of nothing less than of death, and
his wisdom is a meditation not of death but of life' (*Ethics
Pt*. IV. *Prop*. LXVII). This famous sentence emerges
directly from the argument and is certainly not rhetorical
ornament. The proof provided is very simple: 'A free
man, that is, one who lives according to the dictate of
reason alone, is not led by the fear of death (*Ethics Pt*. IV.
Prop. LXIII), but directly desires what is good (*Coroll*. of
same *Prop*.), that is (*Ethics Pt*. IV. *Prop*. XXIV), to act,
to live, and preserve his being on the basis of seeking what
is useful to him. And therefore he thinks of nothing less
than of death, but his wisdom is a meditation of life.
Q.E.D.' (*Ethics Pt*. IV. *Prop*. LXVII. *Dem*.). The free
man is wholly absorbed in the development and exercise
of his own powers of mind and body, and is always aware
of his status as a finite mode of Nature. As he becomes less
and less affected by passive emotions, and in proportion as
his knowledge increases, he becomes more and more
identified in his own mind with the whole process of

Nature: the order of his ideas approximates more and more closely to the order of ideas which constitutes God's thought; he becomes progressively detached from his particular interests as a particular person interacting with a particular environment, and he comes to view all things *sub specie aeternitatis*. His real happiness (*beatitudo*) consists in this contemplation of the whole machinery and system of Nature, and in reflecting within his own mind the whole common order of things. Pain and evil cannot affect him, unless his understanding is imperfect, and unless he is affected by external causes which he does not fully understand. The wise man, pursuing, as all men must pursue, his own preservation and happiness, removes every obstruction to the development of his own understanding; he will need mutual aid, friendship and an ordered society, and he will do what is necessary to promote them. Ideally he requires a community of these secular saints, of disinterested philosopher-scientists bound together by 'the love which acknowledges as its cause freedom of mind' (*Ethics Pt.* IV. *Appendix, Section* XIX); but, the human condition being always imperfection, he will have to accept and sustain the compromise of a system of law and punishment, which for perfectly wise men would be unnecessary. A wise man is still only a man, and therefore only relatively wise and (by definition) not perfect or all-powerful; he cannot be wholly free, rational, and self-contained. 'Human power is greatly limited and infinitely surpassed by the power of external causes, and therefore we do not have absolute power of adapting things which are outside for our use. But we shall bear with equanimity those things which happen to us and which are contrary to what our interest demands, if we are conscious that we have done our duty and cannot extend our actual power to such an extent as to avoid these things, and further, that we are a part of Nature as a whole, and we follow its order. If we understand this clearly and distinctly, that part of us which is called our understanding or intelligence, that is, the best part in us, will entirely acquiesce in this, and will strive to persist in this acquiescence. For in so far as we understand, we can desire nothing other than what is necessary, and we cannot entirely acquiesce in anything other than the truth' (*Ethics Pt.* IV. *Appendix* XXXII). In so far as we are intelligent, frustration and the restless emotions cannot occur, because, realizing the necessity of our position, we have no image of how things might be otherwise, and we therefore have no unsatisfied desires and ambitions. We acknowledge, not (as Leibniz suggested) that all is for the best in the best of all possible worlds, but that all must be as it is in the only possible world. The characteristic virtues of the free man, who thus resolutely sees things as they are and who takes an active pleasure in understanding the infinite concatenation of causes, are strength of mind (*fortitudo*) and nobility (*generositas*); nobility is a form of disinterestedness, not unlike Aristotle's supreme virtue of magnificence (μεγαλοπρέπεια), and is a rational disdain of particular interests and of small worldly calculations. Spinoza carefully distinguishes the strength of mind of the free man from the virtues of stoicism; it is not an exercise of will, but rather the intellectual virtue of confronting the facts impassively, without sentiment and without the intrusion of subjective fears and hopes; it is the virtue of objectivity, an acquiescence in the rationally ascertained truth, however personally disagreeable the truth may seem; for any other attitude to experience must seem to the free man merely stupid and childish, like the attitude of someone who kicks a chair because it causes him to stumble.[1]

ETERNAL LIFE AND
THE INTELLECTUAL LOVE OF GOD

God or Nature is a single system, and to come to understand any particular part of it is necessarily to come to understand more of the whole; if we are to understand ourselves and the causes of our own states and reactions, we must in the process come to learn more about Nature as a whole. Spinoza is often represented as a mystical pantheist because of his description of the good life as 'The Intellectual love of God', just as he is often classified as a materialist and positivist by those who have heard of his dictum that all men pursue their own preservation, power, and pleasure; yet his so-called mysticism is as strictly deduced from his logical and metaphysical premises as is his so-called materialism. The 'Intellectual love of God', in spite of its associations with Christian and other mysticisms, is intended to be a notion with a more definite and mundane meaning, and is something more than the fine

[1] The author's British Academy lecture *Spinoza's Idea of Freedom* (Oxford University Press, 1960) develops the argument more fully

phrase which was to inspire Shelley and Coleridge. It is simply and plainly explained in *Proposition* XXIV of Part V of the *Ethics* – 'The more we understand individual things, the more we understand God.' To understand God must mean to understand Nature, self-creating and self-created; at the third and highest level of intuitive knowledge every individual detail of the natural world is shown as related to the whole structure of Nature; the more we take pleasure, as philosophical naturalists, in tracing in detail the order of natural causes, the more we can be said to have an intellectual love of God. It is perhaps difficult for those educated in the main Christian tradition, with its fundamental contrast between the spiritual and the natural world, to attach to the phrase 'The intellectual love of God' the sense which it must bear in Spinoza's philosophy; for the phrase immediately suggests some purely spiritual, other-worldly contemplation and a detachment of interest from the actual material world. But if one remembers that 'Nature' is, here as elsewhere in Spinoza's philosophy, substitutable for 'God', one sees the 'intellectual love of Nature' as a phrase with altogether different, and no less familiar, associations; there certainly have always been scientists and artists who, to a greater or less degree, have been sustained by a passionate curiosity and delight in the infinite complexities of Nature. Evident literary expressions of this generalized emotion can be found in Lucretius, Montaigne, Shakespeare, Goethe, Shelley, and in varying degrees in many of the other great writers and artists of the world; and many men have been sustained by this absorbed desire to know and to understand who would never give such a name to their curiosity. To such a temper the individual person, the self, a mere finite mode within Nature, appears as significant only in so far as the individual re-creates in his own mind some part of the self-creative activity of Nature, and thereby transcends his condition as a finite and perishing existence. This he can achieve only in so far as his only interest is in Nature, the system of things as they are; all particular desires or passive emotions must be subordinated to this interest.

Under his definition of love (*Ethics Pt*. III. *Def. Emotions* VI) Spinoza explains that it is a property, though not the essence, of love that the lover should wish to unite himself to the object loved; if therefore someone can truthfully be said to love God or Nature, he wishes to unite or identify himself with God or Nature. In so far as I achieve perfect intuitive knowledge of God or Nature in all its details, the ideas which constitute my mind are identical with the ideas which constitute God's mind – that is, I become united with Nature conceived under the attribute of thought; in so far as I desire genuine or scientific knowledge, I must be said to love God or Nature, in the sense of desiring to be united with God or Nature. It is necessary to stress these logical connexions in Spinoza's description of the life of reason, for the sake of insisting that each word in these apparently mystical propositions in fact has a definite logical place in his system, and that the propositions themselves are, at least in intention, rigidly deduced, and are not inserted for their common-place rhetorical effect. It was Spinoza's intention to *prove* that to be rational is necessarily to love God, and that to love God is to be rational: also to prove that, as I come to understand the causes of my desires and of my loves and hates, these desires, loves and hates necessarily become transformed into the intellectual love of God: also to prove that, the more our interests are purely intellectual and our emotions therefore purely active emotions, the more we have in common with each other, and the more the possibility of conflict between us is diminished. He does not try to establish these propositions solely by appeals to experience and observation; they are directly deduced from his basic definitions of pleasure, pain and desire, taken in conjunction with his metaphysics. The life of reason *must* be as Spinoza describes it, if the universe is to be conceived as a single self-creating system, throughout rationally intelligible, of which human beings are finite modes: this is the claim which a Spinozist must make.

ETERNITY

The possible eternity of the human mind, which Spinoza's commentators have always found great difficulty in interpreting, is no less strictly deduced from his definitions; here again part of the difficulty in interpretation comes from some Christian and other associations of the word 'eternity'; the word immediately suggests an everlasting after-life. Spinoza repeatedly distinguishes between 'eternity' in his own sense of the word and 'everlastingness' (he returns to the point in his *Letters* in answer to misunderstandings); 'after-life', or 'survival-after-physical-death', are expressions without any clear meaning in his philosophy. His use of the word 'eternity' cannot be understood without recalling that fundamental distinction between the infinite and the finite on which his whole metaphysics rests. 'By Eternity I understand existence itself, in so far as it is conceived to follow necessarily from the mere definition of an eternal thing. For the existence of a thing, as an eternal truth, is conceived to be the same as its essence, and therefore cannot be explained by duration or time, although a duration may be conceived to be without beginning or end' (*Ethics Pt.* I. *Def.* VIII and *Expl.*). In other words, to say of something that it is eternal is not simply to say that it has or had no beginning and end, or that it is everlasting; it is to say that no temporal predicates or tenses or time determinations of any kind can in principle be applicable to it. The distinction between that which is eternal and that which has duration, whether definite or indefinite duration, is logically involved in the distinction between the infinite and finite; to say of God that he is infinite and eternal is to say that it is meaningless to conceive God as beginning to exist or as ceasing to exist, or as possessing some attributes at one time and not possessing them at another. His essence involves existence, in the sense that the questions 'Does he exist?' or 'When did he come into existence?' are meaningless, just as it would be senseless to ask when the three angles of a triangle became equal to two right-angles. Since 'God or Nature' means (among other things) 'the sum and system of all that is', it must be meaningless to raise questions about the duration of God or Nature's existence; for, in order to attach meaning to such questions, one would need to assume the existence of something external to God or Nature by reference to which God's duration could be determined. Only finite existents can significantly be conceived as enduring for a definite or indefinite length of time; it cannot be included in the essence or definition of a finite thing that it must exist, since it is never self-contradictory to suppose its destruction by an external cause; but the coming into being or the passing away of an infinite substance is inconceivable, because, as part of the meaning of 'infinite', no external cause of such a change can be conceived; only to created things, as opposed to an eternally self-creating substance, can time-determinations be applicable. The notion of an eternal substance is one that can be grasped only by pure reason and not by imagination; we can understand the logical necessity of such a substance, as by pure reason we can understand the geometrical notion of a point having position but no magnitude; but in neither of these cases can we imagine or picture anything corresponding to the notion. In conceiving the notion of something infinite, we must, in order to understand the notion of 'eternity', make the effort of discarding our ordinary imaginative mode of thinking; an unphilosophical mind cannot understand what cannot be imagined or pictured in sensory images, and therefore will always tend to confuse 'infinite and eternal' with 'everlasting'.

All our ordinary time-determinations, our tenses and temporal predicates such as 'past' and 'present' are merely 'aids to the imagination' (*auxilia imaginationis*), and they will not occur in expressions of the highest grade of knowledge; for at the highest level of knowledge Nature is presented *sub specie aeternitatis*; Nature must be understood, not as a temporal sequence of events, but as a logical sequence of modifications necessarily connected with each other. Instead of one event following another in the temporal sense of 'follow', one modification of Nature is shown to follow necessarily from another in the logical sense of 'follow'; it is a timeless, logical necessity that the order of nature should be what it is, in the same sense that it is a timeless, logical necessity that the three angles of a triangle should equal two right angles. In so far as the ideas which constitute my mind add up to such a logical sequence of ideas, reflecting the true order of Nature, my mind becomes part of the infinite idea of God (*infinita idea Dei*); so far and under these conditions, my mind is itself eternal. The difficulty of understanding this doctrine arises from the ordinary use of the word 'mind', a usage which suggests that the mind is a persisting thing or quasi-substance to be distinguished from the succession of ideas which are 'in the mind'; but in Spinoza's terminology an individual mind is merely a particular set of ideas reflecting, more or less adequately or logically, a particular set of modifications of Nature conceived as extension, these latter constituting what is called my body; there is no persisting thing or quasi-substance, 'the mind', which is distinguishable from the ideas of the modifications of my body. The possible eternity of the human mind cannot therefore be intended by Spinoza to mean that I literally survive, as a distinguishable individual, in so far as I attain genuine knowledge; for in so far as I do attain genuine knowledge, my individuality as a particular thing disappears and my mind becomes so far united with God or Nature conceived under the attribute of thought. We feel and know that we are eternal in so far as we conceive things *sub specie aeternitatis;* for we then know our ideas to be eternal truths, and so we know that we are in our thought 'playing the immortal as far as is possible for us', in Aristotle's phrase. In our intellectual life, at the more successful moments of completely disinterested, logical thought, we have these glimpses of the possibility of living, not as finite and perishing modes of Nature, but identified or 'united' with God or Nature as a whole. We at least know what it would be like to transcend the normal human condition of understanding ourselves and the Universe only from a limited and partial point of view; the free man's intellectual love of God is the enjoyment of this identification or union of ourselves with Nature through reason and the understanding; and this identification we never completely and permanently achieve, but must always pursue.

It cannot be claimed that we can easily understand what exactly Spinoza meant when he wrote: 'The human mind cannot be absolutely destroyed with the body, but something of it, which is eternal, remains' (*Ethics Pt.* V. *Prop.* XXIII): certainly part of the explanation is to be found in the proposition 'The mind conceives nothing under the form of eternity (*sub specie aeternitatis*), save so far as it conceives the being of its own body under the form of eternity, that is, save so far as it is eternal' (*Ethics Pt.* V. *Prop.* XXXI. *Dem.*). It seems – but this must be conjectural – that we sometimes have experiences of complete and intuitive understanding, and that on such occasions we feel and know ourselves to be mentally united or identified with the eternal order of Nature; so far we know ourselves to be, in respect of that part of the life of our minds, eternal. This seems to be the ancient doctrine that the life of pure reason, of which we have occasional glimpses, is *another kind of existence*, utterly different from our ordinary life with its local and temporary attachments, and that it is senseless to speak either of decay or of prolongation in respect of this superior existence, in which all our experience is the enjoyment of eternal truths. But everyone must be left further to interpret these propositions as he can, or perhaps to confess that at this point he finds himself beyond the limits of literal understanding; it would be the work of a much longer study to show exactly where the limits of understanding may be expected to fall when we try to talk of the eternity of the human mind.

CHAPTER FIVE

Politics and Religion

SPINOZA, in spite of his debt to Thomas Hobbes, was scarcely less original as a political philosopher than as a metaphysician; and his approach to politics is to-day entirely intelligible and appears as an anticipation of methods which have become familiar in contemporary thought. His conception of political science, which was directly derived from his metaphysics, naturally shocked his contemporaries and successors for the same reasons which made his metaphysics repugnant. He insisted that political and social problems must be studied scientifically and dispassionately, and that moral and religious exhortation, however useful they may be as techniques of government, have no place in political science; if we wish to know how a stable society is to be maintained, we must first understand human beings as natural organisms, and we must not base our policies on ideal conceptions of human nature, or on moral preferences which can only express our subjective tastes and passive emotions. We cannot have a clear and distinct idea of the necessary principles of government unless we first have a clear and distinct idea of 'man and his place in Nature' – that is, unless we have a clear idea of the principles of natural philosophy, including physics and psychology. Secondly, all appeals to supernatural causes or sanctions are expressions of ignorance; whatever happens in human societies happens in accordance with necessary laws, and our only salvation is to understand what these laws are and consciously to adapt ourselves to them. Spinoza repeatedly returns to this appeal for a purely logical and scientific study of human society and of human religion, and for the use of pure reason, the method of clear and distinct ideas, in politics as in every other department of theory and practice. His political works were written with an urgent practical purpose; the superstition which he attacked was a real and present enemy, which had not only disrupted his own life and prevented the publication of his works, but had recently devastated half Europe with religious wars and persecutions. It is not too much to say that, in his own conception, his metaphysics was practically important to the world chiefly as the introduction to his advocacy of reason in ethics and politics; the life of the free and intelligent man, in which alone happiness is to be found, must be for ever unattainable, unless men could be persuaded of the stupidity of religious persecution and of ideological wars. In the *Theological-Political Treatise* he was trying not merely to state the truth for its own sake, but also to persuade; and he was willing to argue popularly in order to be generally understood. As a propagandist of enlightenment, of the liberty of the individual and of freedom of thought, he certainly failed; for he was always a hundred years in advance of his time, and sometimes, as in his Biblical criticism, two hundred years in advance.

In histories of political theory, particularly in English histories, he is often overshadowed by Hobbes, and sometimes appears only as the pupil of Hobbes. The extent of Hobbes' direct influence on him is a matter of inconclusive and largely unprofitable dispute; it was not the practice in the seventeenth century, as it is to-day, always to quote sources and influences (other than sacred or classical authorities), or to provide bibliographies; Hobbes is mentioned by name in the *Letters*, and his works were in Spinoza's library. It can be taken for certain that Spinoza read Hobbes carefully. It is equally certain that, however similar their conclusions in political theory, these conclusions were independently deduced from very different premises. They both argued that all men necessarily seek their own preservation and the indefinite extension of their power and liberty, and they both insisted that this proposition must be the starting-point of political theory; they both regarded peace and security as the end which all men pursue in political associations; peace and security can be maintained, and a war of all against all avoided, only by the vesting of superior power and superior means of coercion in some particular person or group of persons. Power, and not some moral notion, must be the fundamental concept in the study of societies and of the causes of their decline; all political policies must be judged by their effects on the distribution of power within the state, and by the effect of any particular distribution of power in avoiding anarchy, which is always for all men the greatest of evils. In recommending this amoral or naturalistic approach to all political problems as the only possible approach, Hobbes and Spinoza are so far in complete agreement; to both of them appeals to ultimate moral notions or to supernatural sanctions seemed a superstitious or dishonest playing with words. It is strictly meaningless to suppose that men have moral rights or duties, when men are conceived as natural objects and without relation to the particular societies of which they are members; conceived as natural objects, each necessarily pursuing what seems to him the means of his preservation and liberty, they can only be said to have the right to do whatever they have the power to do. If we refuse to acknowledge their right to do something which they are able to do, the refusal is to be justified only by reference to the conventions of their particular state or society; and their submission to these conventions in its turn will be justified by their overriding interest in the maintenance of society and in the avoidance of anarchy. To justify any moral or political decision to anyone must always be to show that the decision makes for his safety and happiness, either immediately or in the long run; no other kind of argument could be relevant.

So far Hobbes and Spinoza are in agreement; they were neither the first nor the last to argue that moral precepts and supernatural sanctions can and should be excluded from political arguments, and that all men in the last resort pursue what they conceive to be their interest, however deviously and ignorantly; this is one of the permanent or recurrent patterns of political theory; it is a point of view represented by sophists and sceptics in Plato's dialogues and more than ever commonplace in the twentieth century. What is more distinctive of Hobbes and Spinoza is the argument that political consent and obedience can be justified as rational self-interest if, and only if, obedience can be shown to be the acceptance of the lesser of two evils, anarchy and insecurity being always the greater evil. All rational political argument must involve the calculation of the lesser of two or more evils from among the practical possibilities; the fundamental mistake of theorists and ideologues is to look for absolute justifications and immutable principles; the defence of abstract principles, whether religious or purely moral, leads to irresoluble conflicts, but rationally self-seeking men can achieve peace by realistic compromises based on a clear estimate of the strength of their rivals; and peace is the supreme end of political associations. But at this point the agreement between Hobbes and Spinoza ceases; for the reasons, expressed and unexpressed, which led them to make a condition of peace the supreme criterion in all political decisions, were largely different, following the differences in their logic and general philosophy; and the meaning which they attached to 'freedom', and the emphasis they placed upon it, was very different. According to Hobbes a man is free in so far as he can in fact satisfy his desires, whatever these desires may be; to be free is to do what one wants, desires and impulses being mechanically or physiologically determined; the negation of freedom is frustration, whether the frustration is the result of natural causes or is caused by other men. Intelligence in practical matters is simply the calculation of the most efficient means to the satisfaction of natural needs; reason must always be the slave of the passions, which are the effects of physical causes. Both as metaphysician and political theorist, Hobbes was a pessimist, and his philosophy provides no visions of salvation or of the good life; the most that can be achieved by prudence and clear thinking is some temporary shelter from pain and fear; and peace and security is no more than the negative condition of not being persecuted or destroyed. Hobbes generally appears as the pessimistic philosopher of realistic conservatism, the defender of the established order, whatever it may be, against the restless claims of individual ambition and conscience; he upholds order and central organization, so that competition shall not lead to war and death.

The practical tendency of Spinoza's naturalistic approach to politics is so different as to be almost diametrically opposed to Hobbes'. They can be grouped together only so long as one chooses to separate their political from their general philosophy. For Spinoza the exercise of reason is not merely the means to self-preservation and the satisfaction of desire, but constitutes in itself the supreme end to which everything else must be a means; and reason is not, as in Hobbes, the empirical calculation of probabilities, but the reconstruction by logical reasoning of the necessary order of the universe. The criterion by which a political organization is to be judged is whether it impedes or makes possible the free man's rational love and understanding of Nature. This is a much wider criterion than Hobbes', involving a less negative conception of security and freedom, and it associated Spinoza with the enemies of authoritarianism. As the necessary consequence of his general philosophy, he was an early advocate of the great liberal conception of toleration and freedom of thought. In interpreting Spinoza's political theory, as in interpreting his moral theory, one must both maintain the balance and show the connexion between his harshly scientific and amoral starting-point and his idealistic vision of a free society; there is always a tendency for the determinist to obscure the idealist, or for the idealist to obscure the determinist.

All men are striving to increase their own pleasure and vitality, but they must recognize that mutual aid is necessary for their survival; nothing is so useful to a man as other men. They therefore find themselves entering into the written and unwritten compacts which are the cement of society. Any law or social convention can, in the nature of things, be observed and obeyed only as long as it seems expedient to the people concerned to obey it; its claim to my allegiance disappears as soon as it ceases to contribute, directly or indirectly, to my safety and happiness. A society remains safe as long as the persons having an interest in supporting its laws or conventions are, or seem to be, more powerful than those having an interest in overthrowing them. The mere existence of a social convention or law cannot either add to or subtract from my natural right, founded on the most elementary necessity of nature, to consult only my own safety and happiness. Spinoza at this point goes even further than Hobbes in refusing to attach any meaning to the words 'right' and 'duty' in their purely moral sense; he is more consistent in regarding the laws and conventions of a society or state as deriving their authority and claim to obedience solely from their usefulness in serving the essential interests of the individuals concerned; as soon as a particular law or convention ceases to safeguard, or begins to threaten, the safety or happiness of a particular individual, that individual is thereby released from any obligation to conform to it; the mere fact that he had previously undertaken to conform to it does not constitute a binding obligation which overrides his personal needs and interests; for nothing can ever, either in principle or in practice, override these needs and interests.

Spinoza's analysis of political consent is easily misunderstood because he persists in using words like 'right' and 'obligation' in a purely non-moral, and therefore unfamiliar, sense; it is paradoxical to say that everyone has a right to disregard a contract solemnly made as soon as it becomes disadvantageous; according to some well-established uses of 'right', this statement is a contradiction in terms. It must be remembered that no moral terms, in the ordinary sense of 'moral', have any place in Spinoza's terminology, since such moral terms in their ordinary connotation are applicable only to human beings, conceived as free agents and not as causally determined natural objects. His analysis is less misleadingly expressed when the word 'right', with its obstinately moral associations, is omitted altogether, and 'power' is substituted; for, although he explicitly defines 'right' in terms of 'power', it is very easy to overlook this re-definition, simply because it is contrary to ordinary usage; as soon as 'right' is replaced by 'power', the argument becomes a clear positivistic analysis of the reasons for obedience to authority.

Contracts, treaties, promises, and oaths of allegiance are in themselves no more than words; but, in any state or organized society, there will necessarily be individuals who possess certain powers of coercion and enforcement; unless someone actually possesses the means of coercion and can in fact make his will effective against all opposition, there must be a state of anarchy and no stable society exists. The actual testable power of this sovereign person, or group of persons, is the sole and sufficient justification of his or their authority and of their claim to obedience. As soon as it is shown in experience that the sovereign authority has in fact lost its power to subdue opposition and to make its will effective, it thereby forfeits its authority as sovereign; all appeals to constitutions or to contracts are irrelevant; the legitimacy of an authority cannot be separated from its effectiveness in action. The sovereign serves my interests as a member of society simply because he is sovereign in fact and action, and only as long as he remains so; he serves my interest, because the fact of his overwhelming power prevents anarchy and insecurity. In the natural state of anarchy and outside an organized society, my power and freedom are limited by my fear of attack by others, and by my natural inability to supply all my own needs and wants; I in effect choose the lesser evil, a smaller loss of power and freedom, when within a civil society I submit to the restraints imposed by the sovereign authority. Within an organized society I am protected against violence and, by mutual aid and the proper division of labour, my natural needs and wants are supplied. Only under extreme provocation can it be reasonable to revolt against the civil authority in defence of my personal interests or loyalties; for the loss of the peace and security of civil society nearly always involves a greater loss of my power and freedom than is involved in any possible alternative, however disagreeable. There may be extreme cases in which the sovereign power tries to coerce me into doing 'things abhorrent to human nature' and in which it directly threatens my life; under such conditions revolt may be the lesser evil. But the ordinary limitations on my power and freedom, which the law with its threats and penalties imposes, are accepted by the reasonable man, as long as the authority imposing the laws proves itself effective in eliminating armed opposition and in keeping the peace. The person or persons who possess sovereign power will naturally seek to extend their power and liberty of action as far as they can without provoking a revolt powerful enough to dislodge them; if they are reasonable men, they will calculate at what point they must restrain the exercise of their power in order not to provoke an effective body of their subjects into revolt; this is the proper art of government. When the sovereign authority becomes so oppressive as to create sufficiently numerous and powerful enemies, it will in fact have ceased to be the sovereign authority; a landslide of disobedience will begin, as the members of the society observe that effective power is beginning to pass into other hands.

The argument by which Spinoza justifies obedience to civil or state authority as reasonable is essentially the same argument as that by which in this century obedience to international authority is generally commended; it is the familiar argument of 'collective security', which is an appeal to enlightened self-interest. The only method of avoiding war, whether between individuals or nations, is to gather a group of individuals or of nations which will in fact possess sufficient force to deter any potential aggressor. The internationalists who used this argument assumed that all nations in fact pursue the indefinite extension of their own power and freedom of action; their starting point was the same as Spinoza's. It is in the interest of any nation to accept the decisions of the international authority, even if this involves some sacrifice of national sovereignty and independence, in order to avoid the greater loss of power and freedom which is involved in war and in the fear of war. Therefore the first aim of a rational foreign policy must be to ally oneself with that group of nations which is powerful enough, if acting together, to constitute an international authority; and generally one must uphold its decisions, even when, considered individually and on their merits, its decisions are repugnant; for anything is better than a relapse into war and the fear of war. It is irrational to resist the edicts of the international authority, even when they involve some limitation of purely national sovereignty, except in the extreme case of these edicts threatening the very survival of the nation.

This familiar and respectable argument is pure Spinozism, applied to international society instead of to civil society. The old contrast between the state of nature and civil society seems remote and artificial to modern readers, because the central power of the nation-state is now generally taken for granted as necessary and unavoidable. The problem of sovereignty, and of the justification of surrendering power to a central authority, comes alive again as soon as it is transposed into terms of international politics; the same egotistic or amoral calculations of profit and loss in the surrender of freedom are invoked, as were formerly invoked in the justification of the authority of the nation-state. The strength of this form of political argument is that it does not rest on changing and disputable moral notions, and can therefore be used persuasively in all circumstances and at all times.

It was Spinoza's purpose to persuade people to think realistically and rationally about political problems, and to discard moral and religious prejudices. He was not analysing how the ordinary man does in fact make political decisions, but recommending a scientific method, which in fact only the relatively rational man actually uses. It is irrelevant to object, as so many commentators have objected, that his political philosophy is not in accordance with ordinary language or with our established ways of thinking about politics; so far from being an objection, this would seem to Spinoza a confirmation. Most men are necessarily governed by passive emotion; they have no clear and objective understanding of the laws which govern the behaviour of human beings in society; if they in fact had such an understanding, positive coercion and the concentration of power in the hands of the government (*imperium*) would be unnecessary, because it is only their passive emotions which lead men into conflict with each other.

Spinoza's conception of society as being always a balance between forces of self-assertion was remarkable as an anticipation of a modern, scientific approach to sociology and politics; the idea of understanding society objectively as a balance of forces was in the seventeenth century largely original, involving an escape from Utopian or Utopian-religious conceptions of a perfect common-wealth or of divinely sanctioned authority. The rational man will study society and its necessary laws of motion as he will study any other natural system, in order to control his human, no less than his natural, environment. He will accept the undeniable fact that governments seek the indefinite extension of their own power and dominion; accepting them as they are, he will try to achieve a stable adjustment of conflicting interests, showing the ruling authority the folly of making enemies of its citizens by oppression, and showing the citizens the folly of risking anarchy for the sake of retaining minor liberties. Although Spinoza naturally respected Machiavelli, as having written of the technique of government in a secular and scientific spirit, he was not himself a Machiavellian. It was the originality, and also perhaps the limitation, of Machiavelli that he conceived politics wholly as the practical art of obtaining and preserving state-power *as an end in itself;* it is this revolutionary conception of political power as in itself the natural and sufficient end of government which has made Machiavelli so significant as an interpreter of political movements for the twentieth century, in which purely Machiavellian government has been realized on a vast scale. Spinoza, by birth a perpetual exile and by temperament a recluse, always a scholar and an individualist, was very remote from the politics for politics' sake of sixteenth-century Italy; for Spinoza the art of government, no less than the reasonable obligations of citizenship, have to be taught and learnt only as a means to an end, the end being the security and comparative freedom of the rational man; for Machiavelli the individual citizen is the raw material of government, from which the ruler must manufacture state-power; Machiavelli writes always from the point of view of government, and of government as a game at which one may succeed or fail, while Spinoza writes from the point of view of the individual, for whom a government and an ordered society are an indispensable means to freedom, or rather a safeguard against anarchy and oppression. It is from this point of view that he reviews the various forms of political organization – monarchy, aristocracy and democracy; what distribution of power is most likely to avert anarchy with the least cost to essential individual liberties? It is a matter of devising a system of checks and balances, of devising incentives and restraints playing on the desire for power and the fears of rulers and ruled, in order to produce the most stable combination of freedom and organization.

The review in the *Political Treatise* of type-forms of monarchy, aristocracy, and democracy follows the pattern originally established by Aristotle. It is introduced by some sentences which immediately show why these abstract Aristotelian discussions of the ideal constitution – a traditional form of political writing at least until the end of the eighteenth century – now seem so unreal and sterile. 'I am fully convinced that experience has revealed all conceivable forms of commonwealth, which are consistent with men's living in unity, and equally the means by which a multitude may be guided and kept within fixed bounds. So that I do not believe that we can by meditation discover in this matter anything not yet tried and ascertained, which shall be consistent with experience or practice. . . . It is hardly credible that we should be able to conceive of anything serviceable to a general society, that occasion or chance has not offered, . . .' (*Political Treatise, Ch.* I, *Sect.* III). No political theorist could to-day write such sentences, suggesting that there is a finite set of possible political structures and that all the possible combinations have already been tried; yet it still seemed natural in the seventeenth century to think in these terms, as it had seemed natural to the Greeks and Romans. An intellectual revolution, comparable in its effects with the rise of mathematical physics in Spinoza's century, has intervened and has destroyed this classical form of discussion of political constitutions, as though they were chemical compounds, which can be designed and brought into being by a right mixture of elements. The barrier between the twentieth-century reader and Spinoza at this point is the conception of historical change which is associated with the methodical study of history; this is something which neither Spinoza nor Hobbes nor any philosopher of their age fully envisaged; the revolution in political theory effectively begins in the next century with Montesquieu; but the historical approach to politics has become so much part of the accepted background of our ordinary thinking that it is difficult to isolate its elements and to state clearly what it involves. Spinoza, like Aristotle and most of the great political philosophers before Vico and Montesquieu, conceived the disintegration of societies, and the constant change of their social and political structure, as something accidental to them, and as signs only of their imperfect design; it seemed at least theoretically possible to design a society which would be static, and in a state of equilibrium, like a closed mechanical system. Historical change, the coming into being and passing away of societies, ought ideally to be avoidable; one could imagine, either in a past

Golden Age or in a future Utopia, a perfectly stable society precisely adjusted to unchanging human needs or to divine purpose. It is only a fall from grace, for a theological thinker, or natural human folly, for a secular thinker like Spinoza, which make for perpetual change and instability in human societies; ideally, as Plato had tried to show, there should be no change in human societies, and in this sense there should be no history. It was the proper work of the political theorist to describe the timelessly ideal constitution to which actual constitutions might be made to approximate as nearly as imperfect human nature allows; it seemed possible and profitable to discuss ideal constitutions without referring to any set of historical conditions on which their existence and appropriateness depends. The revolution in political thought came with the suggestion that historical change, and the decay of political and social structures, is an essential condition of human life, that a state of equilibrium is unthinkable, and that all social systems change into new forms as part of the natural process of human development. As soon as one thinks in terms of unending development, one tends also to think of historical change as an irreversible process, and of each successive set of social and political conditions as without any exact and useful precedent; it then seems senseless to discuss political structures and constitutions abstractly, and without reference to a particular set of historical conditions. In fact almost everybody to-day thinks of political and social changes as incidents in the continuous and irreversible process of history; so far from thinking, like Spinoza, that all the possible political structures have already been imagined or tested in experience, we tend to expect wholly new social and political structures to come into existence in the future, as a result of conditions which we cannot now foresee. To the modern historical mind it seems in principle absurd to try to arrest the process of history by the invention of a finally satisfactory constitution; the problem seems mis-stated, and it seems useless to separate the comparative study of institutions from a historical study of the conditions in which these institutions are to function; for institutions are no more than accepted habits of human behaviour; they are not some kind of inhuman machinery, having a power of their own.

The comparative lack of the idea of history, in the modern sense, in Spinoza's political thought is not accidental, a mere personal defect, but is the essential reflexion of his general philosophy; and the rationalist philosophy of the seventeenth century as a whole cannot be understood unless this neglect of historical method is seen to be involved in it; it is the consequence of taking mathematical physics as the single ideal pattern of genuine knowledge. Nature, necessarily including human nature, was conceived by Spinoza as a system which could be adequately represented in ideas as a deductive system of the kind which the mathematical physicists were trying to provide; all natural events can be shown to be modifications of the single substance, and are to be understood by reference to the eternal attributes and their infinite and eternal modes. Within this systematic knowledge, dates and time-determinations have no place, just as they have no place in geometry; we ordinarily think of the world as a mere succession of events, in the manner of the historian, only because we have not yet arrived at the eternal truths which present the true order of Nature as an eternal system. Such a conception of genuine knowledge, of which analytical geometry seems to have been the first model, clearly allows no place for history as a branch of genuine knowledge of the higher grade; any arrangement of events in a temporal sequence, linked perhaps by the notion of cause in some loose sense of the word, must represent one of the lower grades of knowledge. History, whether human history or natural history, must always be replaced, as knowledge advances, by a logical system of necessary laws; the mere conjunction of descriptions of events, without any logical connexion between the descriptions, must disappear. This programme of science lies behind Spinoza's metaphysical proposition that time is a mode of imaginative, as opposed to intellectual, thinking; in a rationalist philosophy, in which by definition only mathematical knowledge, logically guaranteed, is genuine knowledge, the historical outlook and method can have no proper place. Political theory, no less than physical or psychological theory, must be reduced, as nearly as possible, to a system of necessary and timelessly valid laws or principles; irreversible change and development in time cannot be attributed to Nature when it is conceived as a complete, perfect and eternal system; it is only to our partial and inadequate apprehension that natural processes appear as a mere temporal sequence of events, without any rationally intelligible link between them. As our knowledge of human societies advances, we shall understand them as systems of forces constantly interacting with each other, like more familiar dynamical systems, in accordance with necessary laws. The historical process, the apparent irreversible development in time, will appear as no more than the sum of the interactions among finite modes of Nature, interactions which represent no historical development of the system as a whole; for human societies are no more than highly complicated natural objects.

It is difficult now to recapture the state of mind in which the universe was conceived as essentially a static system, subject to internal modifications and re-distributions of energy according to fixed laws, but not itself developing or essentially changing in time. Even apart from the historical study of human societies, biology and cosmology have made the notion of development in time seem essential to the understanding of Nature in a way which was not foreseen by Descartes, Leibniz, or Spinoza. Samuel Alexander's pertinent criticism of Spinoza was that, in common with most metaphysicians before Whitehead and Alexander himself, he had failed to 'take time seriously'; this, although true, is a dark saying, until we understand how this mysterious oversight in metaphysics shows itself in practical application, that is, in the particular recommendations for the advancement of knowledge which

Spinoza makes; it shows itself, most clearly, I think, in his discussion of political and social structures without reference to historical development, and in his confident assertion that all the essential forms of human society have already been revealed. In common with most political theorists before the nineteenth century, he seems to us now to have greatly under-estimated the time-scale in human history; he had no real knowledge of primitive societies or of the evolution of man, and he could not foresee the effects of the industrial revolution and of modern technology in so rapidly changing human nature and the conditions of life in society; he did not envisage how far human beings had evolved from their original state, or how far and, above all, how rapidly, they were still to evolve. His perspective extended from the Old Testament Jews and the Greeks of the classical world to the seventeenth-century men of science, and all that he could envisage of human nature and human society was included within this span. What is remarkable is that, in spite of the occasional provincialism of tone, he understood so much; the provincialism is most evident in the discussion of constitutions in the *Political Treatise*, and for the modern reader the value of the *Treatise* is to be found rather in the general reflections on political aims and behaviour than in the naive discussion of different constitutions.

Spinoza's general philosophy led him to regard, first, the security and, secondly, the intellectual freedom of the subject as the criterion of a satisfactory government and social structure; to achieve these two supreme ends it is reasonable for the individual to sacrifice his lesser liberties and interests. A slave is someone who obeys an authority or government which is not acting in his interest; but any government or authority which, for reasons of its own, is concerned to guarantee the physical safety and the intellectual freedom of its subjects is a legitimate authority; it is reasonable for the free man to obey such an authority, since it is supplying the necessary conditions of his freedom and happiness. Spinoza anticipates the liberals and radicals of the following centuries in the supreme value which he attaches to individual liberty, and to freedom of thought and religious toleration; if these are sacrificed to state power, the most essential interests of the individual, other than his mere physical safety, have been sacrificed. Spinoza, unlike Hobbes, could not have allowed any compromise with totalitarianism in any of its modern forms, because totalitarianism is inimical both to perpetual peace and to freedom of opinion; and he was necessarily the enemy of any government which tries to impose any doctrinal orthodoxy, whether religious or secular. His own experience, and the experience of his century, was of continuous religious persecution; but his anti-clericalism went further than a conviction that religious persecution must always be stupid and ineffective. Any use of political power and coercion to enforce belief of any kind, whether religious or scientific, must be pointless; for men can be compelled to behave in certain ways, by threats and rewards, but they cannot be compelled to believe; secondly, it is not only impossible but also unnecessary for any government to try to regulate the beliefs of its subjects; it is enough for the purposes of government that citizens should in word and action respect the institutions and conventions of the state. If it can be shown that some of its subjects are expressing opinions the effect of which is to undermine the authority of the government, the government has the natural right to defend itself by suppressing such expressions of opinion, if it has the power to do so; to say that it has the 'natural right' is to say that suppression under these conditions would generally be a reasonable defence of its own interests. What is unreasonable and contrary to natural right is the imposition of opinions or ideologies for their own sake; for such an attempted imposition must always fail in its purpose and must always be liable to provoke resistance. Spinoza discusses in a very modern spirit what is still one of the most acute, and often muddled, problems of politics: namely, the drawing of the line between suppression of expressed opinions which subvert the social order and threaten peace and security, and the positive imposition of orthodoxies; it is still found in practice to be a difficult line to draw, and, being unfamiliar with the more refined modern means of propaganda, he perhaps oversimplifies the problem. Within the experience of his time, the greatest enemies of freedom of thought were the churches and priests, exploiting the fears and the consequent fanaticism of their followers, and using their spiritual authority to extend their temporal power; they were trying to use political power, once achieved, to impose orthodox opinions. It therefore seemed the first aim of a free man's policy to separate state power from the dogmatic pretensions of any church, and to insist that the state should concern itself only with outward conformity to its regulations and conventions, and not with the doctrinal basis of morals; only if it is shown in practice that a particular sect, Jewish, Christian, or Moslem, is liable to disturb the peaceful conduct of affairs, can it be expedient and necessary to proscribe it. The government's interest must be to foster any religion which in fact leads its believers to behave as reasonable and orderly citizens, and to discourage any religion which leads its followers to be aggressive and troublesome; the doctrinal basis of their conduct is a matter of indifference to a reasonable government. Because in his experience churches and priests were the interested enemies of intellectual freedom, Spinoza required state authority to control the churches and priests in the interests of a minimum state religion, which would inculcate certain standards of reasonable behaviour; the religion fostered by the government would be Disraeli's idea of religion, that minimum which all reasonable men could accept. Spinoza did not envisage a situation in which the greatest threat to freedom of thought might seem to come, not from the churches, but from the purely political authorities spreading purely political superstition and fanaticism as a means to extend their own power; he comments incidentally on the peculiar power of governments to persuade, but he did not foresee how far this power might be extended. The first enemy of freedom of thought in the seventeenth century was not centralized government, as in many parts of the world to-day, but the religious authorities, and their power was international; therefore it was Spinoza's concern, as it was Hobbes', to strengthen national governments as a counterweight to the churches. On realistic, non-moral grounds he argued that censorship of opinion must always be both ineffective and unnecessary; any attempt to suppress opinion by law will fail and will bring the law into contempt. The government must always control its subjects by a system of incentives and deterrents, and concentrate solely on the maintenance of peace and order.

The same realistic and amoral principles actually do, and always must, determine foreign policy no less than internal policy. Sovereign states necessarily live in a state of nature with each other, each trying to extend its own power as far as it can, and each concluding temporary alliances for the sake of self-preservation; these alliances are reasonably and properly denounced as soon as it is no longer in the interest of one of the partners to maintain them. To speak of 'gratitude', 'good faith' or 'the sanctity of promises' in such contexts is only playing with words; for it is impossible to expect any government, as it is impossible to expect any individual, to act in such a way as will clearly lead to its own destruction or to the loss of its power. If international order and security are to be created out of anarchy, it can only be by building a combination of forces which can overwhelm any opposition; and this must be achieved by power politics; for all politics at any level is necessarily power politics. Within the perpetual jungle of power politics, the intelligent individual's first aim must be to persuade others to be equally intelligent in the pursuit of their own security; he has a direct interest in freeing others from the passive emotions and from the blind superstitions which lead to war and to the suppression of free thought. But in fact the enlightened and the free are always a minority, and men in general are guided by irrational hopes and fears, and not by pure reason. For these reasons Spinoza, anticipating Voltaire and the philosophical Deists of the next century, admits that popular religions are useful, and that with their childish systems of rewards and penalties they are properly designed to make the ignorant peaceful and virtuous; to the uneducated and unreasoning, morality cannot be taught as a necessity of reason; it must be presented to them imaginatively as involving simple rewards and penalties. The free man therefore will criticize Christian doctrine or orthodox Judaism or any other religious dogma, first, when it is represented as philosophical truth, secondly, on purely pragmatic grounds, if it in fact leads its votaries to be troublesome in their actual behaviour; but to judge and condemn religious faiths by purely rational standards is to misconceive their function. The various religious myths of the world are essentially the presentation in imaginative and picturesque terms of more or less elementary moral truths. The great majority of mankind, who are capable only of the lowest grade of knowledge, will only understand, and be emotionally impressed by, myths which appeal directly to their imagination; the abstractions of purely logical argument mean nothing to them. They cannot understand what is meant by the perfection and omnipotence of God, as a metaphysician understands these ideas; they can understand only in the sense that they may imagine a Being like themselves, but very powerful and very good; they need a story in anthropomorphic terms, and this the popular religions provide.

The dividing-line between religious faith and philosophical truth was, after metaphysics itself, Spinoza's greatest interest; it was a problem which not only involved the whole intellectual history of the Jewish people; it had also dominated his personal life and his own adjustment to the society into which he was born. The *Theological-Political Treatise* lays the foundation of a rational interpretation of the Jewish and Christian religions, and particularly of the Bible; it lays down principles of interpretation of the Bible which were to be further developed with the advent of the Higher Criticism in the nineteenth century. Spinoza avoids many of the over-simplifications and crudities of later rationalist thought, and shows a most precocious understanding of the social function of religious myth. It is almost unnecessary to say that he nowhere shows the slightest personal or nationalistic bias or bitterness, in spite of his excommunication and of his inherited memories of centuries of persecution and fanaticism. Whether he is writing of the nature of prophecy, of miracles, of the allegedly divine origin of Jewish law, or of God's special relation to the Jews, he writes always from the standpoint of pure reason, without personal attachments to any cause or nation, and he applies his irony impartially to the logical evasions of all parties. The non-Jewish reader may forget the background of centuries of Rabbinical interpretation of the Bible and of Jewish history and myth; Spinoza in the *Theological-Political Treatise* is not only a founder of European rationalism, but also one of a long line of Jewish commentators. The tradition of Jewish orthodoxy had been always stricter and more passionately upheld than Christian orthodoxy, and the heresies were fewer and more effectively repressed. Because their persistence as a distinct people through all dispersions and persecution so largely depended on their common religion, the Jews regarded religious deviations as disloyalties which threatened national survival; Spinoza himself remarks the indispensable contribution of religion to the identity of the Jewish people, and interprets parts of the Old Testament as properly to be understood as a figurative illustration of the dependence of Jewish nationality on the Jewish religion; the Bible story of the divine guidance of the Jewish people in their dispersion through the agency of the prophets represents the historical insight that, without prophetic leaders giving them a fanatical sense of mission, the Jews would certainly have lost their sense of national identity. Spinoza's discussion of the relation of philosophy and faith is throughout intermingled with a discussion of the peculiar predicament of his people; for it is their early history and thought which constitute the Old Testament; therefore an understanding of the Old Testament and an understanding of the development of the

Jewish people are for him inseparably connected. This is not the place to consider Spinoza's incidental remarks on the greatness and the limitations of the Jewish people; but his position as a scholar and also a victim of one of the most strictly orthodox communities must be recalled, if only because it is never allowed to cloud his argument; his impartial attitude illustrates his own conception of philosophy and of the free man.

In the Preface to the *Theological-Political Treatise* Spinoza declares the main purpose of the book to be the defence of freedom of opinion; he will show that public order is not only compatible with freedom of opinion, but that it is incompatible with anything else. The argument is a now classical liberal argument, and is still invoked to-day. 'If deeds only could be made the grounds of criminal charges, and words were always allowed to pass free, seditions would be divested of every semblance of justification, and would be separated from mere controversies by a hard and fast line.' If law 'enters the domain of speculative thought', it will not only destroy the possibility of the free life for the individual, but generate those civil disorders which it is the function of law to avert. The argument that 'Revelation and Philosophy stand on totally different footings' and, rightly interpreted, cannot conflict, is a means to showing the absolute necessity of allowing freedom of opinion; the conclusion is that 'Everyone should be free to choose for himself the foundation of his creed, and that faith should be judged only by its fruits; each would then obey God freely with his whole heart; while nothing would be publicly honoured save justice and charity.' The chief document supporting Christian and Jewish revelation is the Bible; therefore a clear method of interpreting the scriptures is required. What was the inspiration of the Jewish prophets? What are we to believe of miracles? In what sense is the Bible the word of God? These are the old questions which many learned and devout interpreters had confused by their subtlety and sophistry, 'extorting from scripture confirmations of Aristotelian quibbles'; they had disregarded the plain meaning of the text in order to reconcile scripture with philosophy, faith with reason. But faith and reason cannot be, and do not need to be, reconciled; on the contrary, they can only be separated, each being allotted its own sphere; while scripture and faith are concerned with the 'moral certainty' necessary to men who cannot reason, philosophy and reason are concerned with logical or mathematical certainty. The Bible shows the prophets to have been ignorant men with vivid imaginations and a powerful and just moral sense; therefore they were suitable leaders of a primitive people; their theoretical opinions are the primitive and mutually contradictory superstitions typical of a pre-scientific age; but an effective prophet does not need to be a philosopher any more than a philosopher needs to be a prophet. The appeal of the prophet is to the imagination, and he must have the means to impress simple, useful moral precepts on ignorant men. The appeal of the philosopher is to the reason, and he is concerned only with the consistency and truth of what he writes, and not at all with its effect on the emotions through the imagination. The work of the prophet is achieved if he persuades men to obey the laws of their society and to lead quiet and useful lives; the form which this persuasion must take, if it is to be effective, must depend on the state of knowledge within the society. If we appreciate the old Jewish prophets from this standpoint, we find that they were ignorant men brilliantly gifted to instil faith and obedience in an ignorant society by myth and story. As philosophers, we understand their function, and do not regard their writings as making any claim to literal truth. Confusion comes from the false sophistication of those who, like the great Maimonides, try to read philosophic truths into the text of Scripture by ingenuities of interpretation. It is both futile and dangerous to try to convert the old prophets into rational metaphysicians; one will only undermine their authority as prophets. Any intelligent and pious Jew or Christian must experience a crisis of conscience if he is asked to choose between modern knowledge and scriptural authority; but the crisis is unnecessary, because there can be no question of choosing between reason and prophecy; the dilemma is falsely stated; rational argument requires belief, and religion and prophecy require only practical obedience to moral precept. To require belief in miracles of educated men is gratuitously to provoke disobedience, and this is the very vice which the stories of miracles served, in very different conditions, to prevent. As the only interest of a rational government is the obedience of its subjects, it will permit, and will recognize that it cannot prevent, every variety of belief, provided only that these beliefs are compatible with obedience and good order. Therefore in a free (that is, rationally governed) state 'every man may think what he likes, and say what he thinks': 'The real disturbers of the peace are those who, in a free state, seek to curtail the liberty of judgement which they are unable to tyrannize over' (*Theological-Political Treatise. Ch.* XX). A rational government requires enlightened and tolerant citizens, just as free men require an enlightened and tolerant government. This is the proposition which the *Theological-Political Treatise* was intended to prove; it is shown as the direct consequence of Spinoza's metaphysical conception of a person as a finite mode of Nature, necessarily seeking his own preservation, and potentially free and happy in so far as he can acquire rational understanding of Nature and of himself. Freedom and happiness are within, and virtue is its own reward; the official religions and conventional moralities, in their own interests as in the interests of freedom of mind, must be confined to the externals of human behaviour; they must ensure the social conditions in which true freedom can develop. Spinoza further argued, with little relevance to conditions after the Industrial Revolution, that a restricted 'democracy', with the opportunity of political power limited by a property qualification, was most likely to provide this rational and non-interfering government; his contemporary ideal was the mercantile community of Amsterdam, which provided asylum to people of many creeds and denominations, provided that they were willing to keep the peace. Universities and academies of instruction must be free from state-control, free intelligence rewarded, public business publicly transacted, and the churches disestablished and maintained at the expense of their believers. Then every man may be free to live his own life and extend his own mind, wherein alone lies his happiness, within a neutral framework of common convenience.

CHAPTER SIX

The Nature of Metaphysics

THERE are many ways in which a great metaphysical system such as Spinoza's may be studied and enjoyed; one may appreciate its rigour and consistency very much as a theory in pure mathematics may be appreciated: as a piece of intellectual architecture of which the various parts fit together to form an imposing fabric of abstract concepts. This is certainly not how he himself would have wished his system to be regarded; and such an approach would not bring out its permanent importance as a contribution to philosophy. Secondly, any powerful philosophy presents a peculiar view of the world, and of human experience, which we can come to share, and which we can appreciate and understand without requiring that it should be the only acceptable view, and without raising any sharp questions about the literal truth or falsity of its doctrines. One may learn to view the world and one's own experience in terms of the concepts which Spinoza provides, as one may also learn to think of one's experience in terms of Plato's or of Hume's philosophy. But, however legitimate and illuminating such a literary characterization of a metaphysics may be, it leaves out the hard core of logical argument on which Spinoza, like other great metaphysicians, confidently rested his vast claims; these claims, and the arguments which support them, must be taken seriously, and must finally be accepted or refuted. Lastly, a metaphysical system may be interpreted and judged historically, that is, in relation to the developing sciences, and to the other branches of knowledge, characteristic of the period in which it was written; any metaphysics, which is not purely mystical, will be in part concerned with the limits and possibilities of natural knowledge, and this relation to contemporary science is particularly obvious in the great metaphysical systems of the seventeenth century; these systems are so evidently designed (among other purposes) to prescribe the outlines of a new physical science in opposition to the earlier Aristotelian programmes of natural knowledge. These are three points of view from which metaphysical systems may be understood and appreciated as having a value of their own. But to many twentieth-century philosophers the construction of metaphysical systems of any kind has come to seem finally useless and impossible; some philosophers are even prepared to dismiss all deductive metaphysics of the type of Spinoza's as senseless, on the ground that only by careful experiment and observation can anything be learnt of the actual structure of the universe; a philosopher (it is argued), sitting in his study and elaborating definitions, cannot produce anything more than empty tautologies as he draws out the remote consequences of his own chosen definitions; only the experimental scientist can tell us what actually happens in Nature and so can enable us to understand and to control ourselves and our environment. This firm distinction between metaphysics and experimental science, on which all contemporary empiricism rests, derives largely from Hume and Kant; it is only with an effort that we can now reconstruct the conditions of knowledge in which the dividing line between metaphysics and natural science was not immediately recognized as obvious. We no longer have any need of arm-chair programmes of science; contemporary philosophers are in effect proclaiming this fact when they denounce all metaphysical systems as useless and misleading. But speculation of a kind which may be absurd and useless at one stage in the development of our knowledge may be significant and useful at another; associated with the beginnings of experimental physics, it is natural to find philosophical speculation about the ultimate nature of Matter: associated with the beginnings of experimental psychology, it is natural to find philosophical speculation about the powers and faculties of the Mind; and to-day, at the beginning (it is to be hoped) of a proper empirical and comparative study of the forms of language, we have philosophical speculation about the forms of Language. Experiment replaces speculation, and makes it otiose, as natural knowledge advances; but it does not follow that metaphysical speculation is in itself always useless; it follows only that speculation of a particular kind is discarded when it has finally served its purpose.

But such an historical interpretation and justification of a metaphysical system yields only half its significance, and still does not meet Spinoza's own claims. It is a plain fact that certain large metaphysical questions naturally present themselves to reflective people in almost all periods as being problems which require an answer, and that some of these metaphysical questions are independent of the changing problems of scientific method. Although the formulation of these questions varies from period to period, and although they are often entangled with the more transitory questions of the logic of science, the same perplexities can be recognized as constantly repeating themselves through different disguises; they are called metaphysical questions just because they seem to be for ever outside the scope of any of the special sciences; they seem always to lie on the frontiers of organized knowledge, however far these frontiers may be extended. Empiricist philosophers have been apt to say that, because such metaphysical questions lie outside the possible scope of any of the sciences, they cannot properly be answered. But this is not in itself to remove the perplexity; for the questions are still asked and still found puzzling; and why should it be assumed that all genuine questions must be scientific questions? Some philosophical questions puzzle us because we can neither show why they are unanswerable nor devise a possible method of answering them. Obvious examples of such constant metaphysical questions are – First: How did the Universe begin? Was it created? Must we suppose a Creator? Second: Can the existence and functioning of human will and reason be adequately explained in purely scientific terms? If so, what account can be given of the moral aspirations and purposes of human beings? Third: Is there any single, true and adequate form of description of the external world? Does it even make sense to ask for such a form of description? Of these three representative questions, which almost every great philosopher has in his own way tried to answer, the first is certainly the most important for the understanding of metaphysics in general and of Spinoza's metaphysics in particular. It is a fact of history that the earliest metaphysics, as it first emerges from religious and poetic myth, is generally an attempt to answer these primitive questions about the origins of the universe, rationally and with arguments; such cosmological questions at least seem at first sight to make sense, and there seems no obvious misuse of language involved in asking 'Was the world created out of nothing?' or 'There must have been a First Event: how did it happen or how was it produced?' But as soon as one tries to answer these apparently intelligible questions one is involved in all the irresolute difficulties of various theories of creation, as they are found not only in Christian, Jewish and many other theologies, but also in the cosmologies of paganism.

But there remains another resource, another way of coming nearer to the source of puzzlement, and this is to inquire into the meaning of the questions themselves. Although these questions about the origins of things seem at first sight grammatically clear and intelligible, perhaps they are questions so constructed and interpreted that no answer could ever in principle be accepted as a satisfactory answer; perhaps the questioner has been misled by the familiar form of sentences and has not made clear to himself what kind of answer he wants; perhaps he has not realized that to ask about the origins of the universe is to ask a question which is different in kind from any question about the origins of a particular thing, or kind of thing, within the universe; he may not have realized that it is odd to ask a question about causes and origins, and to be offered in return some purely *a priori* arguments about what *must* have happened at the beginning of things. Questions about causes and origins are ordinarily experimental questions, to be settled by collecting evidence; yet philosophical puzzles about creation do not seem to be settled by astronomical evidence about the origins of the universe; it seems that, whatever empirical discoveries are made, the metaphysical puzzle will still remain; and that is why the problem is called metaphysical; it is characteristic of metaphysical puzzles that they always recede beyond the reach of experimental evidence, however far the evidence may go. The metaphysician may be led, by further probing, to doubt whether any statement about 'The Universe', or 'The totality of things', can be given a sense, and therefore whether any philosophical argument involving these terms can yield anything other than confusion. It is by pressing such doubts as these that philosophers since Hume and Kant have tried to undermine the pretensions of deductive metaphysics. Kant first clearly suggested how apparently insoluble metaphysical questions about the creation of the universe may arise from an illegitimate extension of the use of such concepts as 'Cause' and 'Substance' outside the contexts of matter-of-fact argument for which they were designed; and again in this century attempts have been made to show how we may begin to talk nonsense when we are misled by verbal analogies and begin to use terms so generally – e.g. 'The Universe', 'Nature as a whole', 'The totality of things' – that no statement of which they are the subject can ever be related to any definite context.

It is along these lines of argument that any thorough criticism of Spinoza's metaphysics must proceed. It is not enough dogmatically to assert, as so many empiricist philosophers, from the Greek sceptics to the present day, have asserted, that any statement about the origin and structure of the world must be meaningless if it cannot be tested by experiment; for any such sweeping generalization can itself only be justified by an examination of particular cases. We cannot lay down the limits of intelligibility in the use of language until we have explored beyond these limits; we do not know what we can and cannot ask until we have actually formulated the questions, and until we have tried to attach a sense to the words which they contain. The puzzles can only be removed at the root by careful probing of the use of such expressions as 'The Universe', 'Nature', 'God', 'Cause', 'Substance', 'Creation'. There is no doubt that Spinoza regarded Nature or the world as something the existence of which has somehow to be explained; the mere existence of things of any kind seemed to him to constitute a problem, and a problem which it is the work of the philosopher to solve. The scientist explains the existence and properties of particular things, and kinds of thing, within the universe; but the existence of the Universe itself, or the fact that *anything* exists, seems to the metaphysician to require an explanation of another kind. It seems that the great majority of those who have looked for some explanation of the existence of things in metaphysics, or (more commonly) in revealed religion, have in this respect thought as Spinoza thought. The various sciences provide explanations of particular kinds and classes of natural events and of the interconnections between them; but ought we not to look for some all-embracing explanation of the origin and design of the Universe itself? Spinoza's own explanation, in terms of an infinite, eternal and self-creating substance, is far too subtle, abstract and remote to seem to the ordinary man an intelligible answer to his question; and when compared with simple orthodox doctrines of an act of Creation by a Supreme Being, Spinoza's doctrine might even seem a rejection of the question itself; for his answer is that there *could* not have been an act of creation, or a creator, in any simple sense of the words. But in fact Spinoza did think that he had explained the existence of things in the only way in which the existence of things could be explained. An anti-metaphysical critic would need to show that 'explanation', and the words associated with it (e.g. the word 'cause') have been deprived of all their ordinary meaning in this strange context, in which it is not the existence of some particular things, but of Nature itself, which calls for an explanation; the critic might argue that ordinarily to explain something is to exhibit it as an instance of some more general uniformity in Nature, and that explanation in this sense can have no application when we are speaking of the totality of things; he might take this as an illustration of the general fallacy of regarding the totality of things, or of regarding Nature in Spinoza's sense, as being itself a thing; at this point he would have reached the kernel of Spinoza's philosophy, the point on which almost all the difficulties of interpretation are centred. Spinoza's whole metaphysics is substantially contained in his notion of Nature, as a whole, as the unique substance; as soon as he is granted the use of this notion, together with the traditional connotations of the word 'substance', he is already launched on his way to his final conclusions. What must we suppose if Nature as a whole is to be regarded as completely intelligible? This is the question from which Spinozism begins.

It is characteristic of metaphysical systems, and particularly of the greatest of them, that they can often be shown to rest on the exaggeration, or the taking very seriously, of one or two simple logical doctrines and linguistic analogies; as soon as the underlying logical assumptions are laid bare, the purely intellectual motives of the whole construction become clear. It is this fact (among others) which makes the great metaphysical systems seem permanently instructive, even from the point of view of those who would now dismiss deductive metaphysics as a useless substitute for scientific experiment; most metaphysical systems can be in part interpreted as exaggerated projections upon reality of some obsessive difficulty of logic and of the interpretation of the forms of language. They generally show an obsession with a particular form of expression, or type of discourse, and a determination to assimilate all forms of expression and types of discourse to this single model, whatever it may be. Plato's metaphysical theory of a real world of Ideas or Forms, which he contrasts with the actually perceived world of phenomena, has its logical root (or one of them) in a puzzle about the use of general names and abstract terms: Leibniz's metaphysic of monads, which are ultimate spiritual substances, has its logical root (or one of them) in a puzzle about the distinction between expressions which are used to describe and expressions which are used to refer and to indicate. We may therefore instructively translate a metaphysical doctrine about the ultimate elements of Reality into a logical doctrine about the ultimate elements of our discourse, provided always that this translation is not regarded as an account of the metaphysician's own intentions. There are certain permanent or recurring puzzles about the forms of our knowledge, and also the forms of our language, which lead to metaphysical doubts, and which seem to provide a motive for rejecting common-sense forms of expression; when we brood on these logical puzzles, they make our ordinary, unreflective claims to knowledge seem confused and ill-founded. What is largely new in the philosophy of the last thirty years, and what makes Spinoza's or Leibniz's metaphysics sometimes seem extravagant and remote, is that many philosophers are now satisfied to trace these perplexities to their source in misunderstandings of the common forms of language and to a failure to distinguish between different types of discourse; it is believed that when these misunderstandings of the forms of language have been exposed, the main intellectual motives for metaphysical constructions will have been removed; we shall have used metaphysical doubts, and the examples which the great metaphysical systems afford, mainly in order to gain a further insight into the different forms of our language and into the consequences of neglecting the different uses and functions of these forms; and we will have freed ourselves from the prejudice that all knowledge must conform to a single pattern, and particularly from the prejudice that all genuine knowledge must be of the form of a mathematical demonstration. If the logical germ of Spinoza's system is to be found in the notion of Nature, or the totality of things, as the unique substance, we must first ask what, if anything, we can mean when we talk, as it sometimes seems natural to talk, of 'The Universe', or 'Nature as a whole', or 'The totality of things'. Virtually the same question could be put in another way by asking ourselves what, if anything, we could mean by '*complete* scientific knowledge' or 'perfect knowledge'. All these seem at first sight intelligible phrases which we might normally use even without having any metaphysical argument in mind. As we attach a clear meaning to the growth of scientific knowledge and to knowledge becoming less and less incomplete, it is natural to assume that it makes sense to talk of the limiting case of absolutely perfect knowledge; the natural implication is that we may assess all existing claims to knowledge by reference to this ideal of complete and perfect knowledge. This is the implication followed by Spinoza together with other rationalist philosophers; as every increase in scientific knowledge means that a wider range of phenomena is explained within some theory, or some deductive system, it is natural to infer that absolutely perfect knowledge must mean an intuitive understanding of the whole Universe as represented by a single deductive system, within which everything is explained as necessarily connected with everything else. If it makes sense to talk of Nature as a whole, then it makes sense to talk of the possibility of complete and perfect knowledge; and if it makes sense to talk of the possibility of perfect knowledge, then it makes sense to talk of Nature as a single system. But a logically critical and analytical philosopher may from the beginning suggest doubts about the meaning of both these complementary notions. He may perhaps suggest that, although we can significantly talk of the totality of things *of a certain kind*, we cannot significantly talk of the totality of things, without specifying the defining property of the class of things referred to; anyone using the word 'Nature', as Spinoza uses it, would need to refer to the totality of things in explaining what he means by 'Nature'; and he would thereby be involved in using the word 'thing' as though it were an ordinary class-term. The critical philosopher would need to explain how the use of such formal words as 'thing' and 'event' differs from the use of ordinary descriptive terms such as 'man'; he would hope to show why it is a logical mistake to suppose that we can speak of the class or collection of all *things* as we can speak of the class or collection of all *men*. At this stage the critic would find himself engaged in the long and difficult process of illustrating the different uses of expressions of different categories, with the purpose of showing how metaphysical theories may arise out of grammatical analogies which, when exposed, are finally seen to be misleading. Metaphysics of the type of Spinoza's, which depend on regarding the existence of the universe as a problem requiring some general explanation, illustrate the metaphysician's tendency to ask questions which are so general that no definite sense can be attached to them. We stumble into metaphysical questions by using words such as 'thing' and 'cause' without any of the restrictions on which their normal significance depends.

Such a step-by-step investigation of the use of terms in the metaphysical questions which Spinoza tries to answer lies outside the scope of this book; and only such a step-by-step investigation can enlighten and satisfy anyone who, in sympathy with Spinoza, has ever thought of the existence of the universe as requiring a general explanation, or who has ever entertained the possibility of complete and perfect knowledge. It must be enough here to indicate the general lines of criticism which an analytical philosopher would follow. It is probable that to the great majority of contemporary readers Spinoza's attempt to deduce the true nature of things from a set of definitions will seem unavailing without the need of argument; they may be inclined to reject as unnecessary any detailed dissection of the logical grounds and motives of such metaphysical arguments, holding it to be obvious that no manipulation of definitions can ever yield genuine knowledge of the origin of things or of man's place in Nature; perhaps there is a tendency for many people to be in this sense positivistic without further reflexion. But whatever may be the prevailing common-sense of the time, just this 'further reflexion' is always the proper concern of philosophy. Nothing can be dismissed as nonsense until an honest and thorough attempt has been made to understand it; and understanding must involve uncovering, step by step, the connexion which leads from one proposition to another in the systems and arguments examined. Our patterns of thought and forms of language are constantly changing in response to new needs and new interests; we cannot therefore lay down, once and for all, the limits of intelligible discourse, in such a way as to exclude the asking of questions that are not scientific but are metaphysical; wherever we try from time to time to draw the frontier of scientific inquiry, metaphysical questions will always arise precisely on this frontier. Spinoza's doctrines of God and creation, the freedom of the will, human immortality, and the relation of mind and body, are admittedly not supported by scientific inquiry and observation, but are based on purely *a priori* arguments; but they are attempted answers to questions which in all periods have proposed themselves to reflective people as genuine perplexities, the force of the perplexity in each case being that we cannot yet see how they could possibly be answered, by any experimental method. In asking ourselves to-day about creation and the freedom of the will, we know that we are asking metaphysical questions, in the sense that we know that the major part of the problem in each case is to find how the question could possibly be answered, rather than to find the actual answer by some already agreed method; in each case we are prepared to be convinced, by a careful analysis, that the question asked involves some confusion of thought and of language; perhaps the question can be broken down into two or more different questions, each of which might be susceptible of a definite answer in scientific terms, or perhaps a clear convention on the different uses of words is needed; but until this analysis has actually been done in each case, the questions stand unsolved as metaphysical problems. But for Spinoza and for the majority of his contemporaries, 'philosophy' was a word with a wider sense; all systematized knowledge of the world came under the heading of 'natural philosophy'; the word 'philosophy', by itself, was still the name of any synthesis of human knowledge and opinion in all its departments. As human knowledge develops in range and detail, the word 'philosophy' comes to have a progressively narrower and narrower sense; the large questions, which it originally denoted, become more and more sub-divided and particularized, and the accumulation of all-important detail makes any very general synthesis seem less and less useful; finally all *a priori* syntheses imposed on the multiplicity of different inquiries come to seem inadequate and empty. The more we learn by experiment and observation, the less we are prepared to speculate without experimental evidence, and the more we are inclined to remit every question about human nature, or about the nature of things, for detailed investigation by an expert observer. But from the original amalgam of still confused questions called 'philosophy', there survives always a residue which we cannot yet further break down into simple and clear elements, and in respect of which we cannot yet see how definite knowledge is in principle possible; these are the questions of which the *meaning* is the problem. Astronomy and cosmology, for instance, have made great advances as experimental sciences, and even within the last fifty years much has been learnt of the origin and age of the universe; most *a priori* speculation by philosophers on space, time, matter and physical nature generally, has been discredited, and is now only of historical interest. But however the problem of creation may have been circumscribed and reduced by logical analysis and experimental science, taken together, there still remains some part of the traditional puzzle about the origin of the universe which is puzzling. However cautious and empirical we may become, we will naturally sometimes pause to ask extravagantly general and all-embracing questions about the design of the world and about our place within it, if only because we cannot know what is, and is not, answerable until we have proposed the questions.

But perhaps, in the last resort, no one will fully understand and enjoy Spinoza who has never to some degree shared the metaphysical temper, which is the desire to have a unitary view of the world and of man's place within it.

From this point of view the *Ethics* has no equal in modern European literature. It presents a view of the world, and a way of life appropriate to this view of the world, in a manner which is entirely definite and unambiguous; Hume and Kant are, I think, the only other modern philosophers who provide a natural philosophy and a moral philosophy which are so perfectly complementary and which are, when taken together, complete. Hume and Kant, and in this century Ludwig Wittgenstein, have classically shown by very different forms of argument the limits of human reason, and it is the function of critical philosophy to draw and to re-draw the limits of human reason from changing points of view and in different phases of knowledge. But one must also understand the motives of those who overstep these limits in pursuit of complete and final explanations, since these are the perpetual motives from which philosophy itself arises; and even the most critical may respect and enjoy the extravagant extension of pure reason in its furthest ambition, of which Spinoza is, after Plato, the greatest philosophical example.

Life

APART from the small remnant of his correspondence, there are three sources for the story of Spinoza's life; the editor's short preface to his posthumous works, a short and inaccurate contemporary biography ascribed to Lucas, and a longer and later life by Colerus, based on testimony and reminiscence at second hand. Spinoza deliberately effaced his own personality and wished his philosophy to stand alone. Consequently we possess only a bare outline of reliable fact; but it is just enough to explain why his life and manners so impressed both his friends and his enemies. Knowledge of the personality and circumstances of a philosopher is in general strictly irrelevant to the understanding and evaluation of his arguments. But some great philosophers have also been interesting and exceptional men, and Spinoza is conspicuous among these; the extreme simplicity of his story makes it worth telling, and in itself illustrates his character and purpose.

Spinoza was born in Amsterdam on 24 November, 1632, and died at The Hague on 21 February, 1677. His ancestors were Portuguese crypto-Jews, that is, Jews whom the Inquisition had compelled outwardly to profess Christianity, but who remained in fact faithful to their own religion. In the last decade of the sixteenth century his father and grandfather had left Portugal and sought asylum from religious persecution in Amsterdam; the mercantile communities of Holland were at that time the most tolerant in Europe and the natural centre for refugees from persecution. Amsterdam was full of Jewish faces of the type that Rembrandt painted. Spinoza's family were prosperous leaders of the large Jewish community in Amsterdam, his father being on many occasions warden of the Jewish Synagogue; it was because of the importance of his family that the philosopher's lapse from the orthodox faith was to cause such stir and scandal in the Jewish community, which felt its solidarity centrally threatened. Benedict Spinoza, the first name being the conventionally latinized equivalent of the Hebrew *Baruch*, was first educated in the traditional Hebrew studies, and he spoke Spanish at school; he learnt Portuguese from his father, Latin from a German scholar, and Dutch from his neighbours. He was a Hebrew scholar and author of a Hebrew grammar; and his surviving library shows that he was a continuous reader of Spanish literature of all kinds. Little is known of his early scientific education, or of how he came to choose the highly skilled craft of lens-making as his profession; but it provided him with a livelihood in association with the new sciences, particularly optics, in which he was deeply interested; he could do his intricate work alone and as his own master.

Jewish orthodoxy, like Christian orthodoxy, had been

profoundly shaken by the new ideas of the Renaissance and by the natural philosophy of Galileo, Kepler, Bacon and Descartes. Spinoza grew up among excommunications and recantations and heard at first hand of many violent scenes of religious doubt and persecution. The Jews were not yet citizens in Holland and their leaders feared that the outbreak of free-thought in their community would alarm the Dutch, who had already to contend with every variety of Christian schism sheltering within their borders; Amsterdam had become a centre of small sects and of violent religious discussions in many languages. To Spinoza, as to most strictly educated but critical Jews, the interpretation of the Bible presented an insurmountable obstacle; neither in its literal interpretation nor in the figurative or allegorical interpretations suggested by earlier Jewish philosophers could Biblical doctrine be made compatible with natural science and adult logic; even as a very young man Spinoza was in the habit of acknowledging this incompatibility. Although he had no desire to agitate or to proselytize, he could not be persuaded by bribes or threats to renounce or to conceal his sceptical conclusions. He continued to attend the Synagogue at intervals and he always behaved as a natural member of the Jewish community. But his scepticism was too dangerous to be ignored and warnings were useless; he could not promise to pretend to believe what he did not believe; at the age of twenty-four and three years after his father's death, he was finally excommunicated with all the solemnity and violence of language which is appropriate to such occasions. He was an outcast from the only community to which he naturally belonged.

He quietly set himself to make his own living by himself and without ties; he had typically renounced most of his inheritance after having vindicated his legal right in a lawsuit with his step-sister. From 1656 to 1660 he lived in Amsterdam, grinding and polishing lenses, and discussing Descartes' 'new philosophy' with a group of enlightened and sectarian Christians, who had formed a small circle interested in philosophical problems; he became the admired intellectual leader of this circle, and one of his friends offered to leave him enough money to enable him to live in comfort and to devote himself wholly to philosophy; but he would only accept a very small annuity as a legacy, thinking it better to live with as few possessions as possible and to earn his own living independently as a craftsman. He always avoided the burden of possessions and was naturally ascetic. In 1660 he left Amsterdam for Rijnsburg, a quiet village near Leyden, apparently in order to find solitude for writing; there he wrote his *Short Treatise on God, Man and his Well-being*, the greater part of his geometrically ordered statement of Descartes' philosophy, and probably at least the first draft of the first part of his masterpiece, the *Ethics*. He remained in correspondence with his philosophical friends, and sent them extracts from his writings. In all periods philosophical discussion has depended on the existence of small groups interested in the 'new philosophy' of the time; in the seventeenth century, when travel and publication were less easy and learned societies fewer, the advance of knowledge depended particularly on learned correspondence; the surviving correspondence of Spinoza is small in comparison with that of Descartes and Leibniz, and almost all his correspondents were too far beneath him in understanding; he had the reputation in Europe of being a mysteriously subversive thinker, with whom it was dangerous to associate; and he had deliberately sought shelter from controversy in a small circle, which, even so, was never small enough to exclude fanatics. Perhaps the most distinguished of his correspondents was Oldenburg, who was one of the first two secretaries of the Royal Society in London, and who was therefore at the centre of the intellectual world. It was largely through Oldenburg that Spinoza entered into relations with Huygens and Boyle, and with other scientists of the time. In 1663 Spinoza yielded to the suggestions of his friends, and allowed his exposition of Descartes' philosophy in geometrical order to be published, together with the appendix called *Metaphysical Thoughts*; the introduction by Meyer, a friend of Spinoza's, explained that the volume did not represent the author's own views. It is typical of Spinoza's situation in society that this early exposition of a philosophy in which he did not himself believe was the only work bearing his own name to be published in his life-time. In 1663 he moved to Voorburg, near The Hague; by 1666 the manuscript of the *Ethics* must have been nearly finished, and he began work on the *Theological-Political Treatise*, which was published anonymously in 1670. He had already decided that, in view of his gradually growing notoriety as an atheist, the *Ethics* could not be published while he was alive, even anonymously; the *Treatise*, although it contains a sketch in outline of his metaphysics, was designed as a persuasive defence of toleration and of liberal principles in a modern republic; at least in intention it was a tract for the times. Spinoza never thought of his own, or of any genuine, philosophy as morally neutral or as of purely theoretical interest; he considered himself fully engaged intellectually in what was the greatest public issue of his time, the possibility of freedom of thought in a secular state. On at least two occasions he is said to have intervened actively in politics, and it is not impossible that there were other occasions which have not been recorded; for the publication of the *Treatise* brought him fame in spite of its anonymity. When in 1672 the French invaded Holland and the brothers de Witt were murdered by the mob as appeasers, he tried to protest publicly at the risk of his own life; and an uncertain story represents him as an unsuccessful emissary of the peace party in Holland to the Prince de Condé in 1673. In this same year he declined an invitation from the Elector Palatine to the Chair of Philosophy at the University of Heidelberg; in refusing, he reaffirmed the guiding principle of his life, a principle which was justified by metaphysical argument in the *Ethics*; as a philosopher, he must remain without official commitments, which might prevent him from thinking and from expressing himself freely; as a philosopher he wanted nothing more than the seclusion and tranquillity in which he could extend his own thought to its furthest conclusions without need of compromise; he must always remain utterly independent.

An irritating mystery surrounds Spinoza's relations with Leibniz, the only living man who could wholly have understood his philosophical designs. It is certain that as early as 1671 Leibniz had sent to Spinoza, as a known expert in optics, a tract which he had written on this particular subject; it is also certain that Leibniz stayed at The Hague in 1676, and we have it on his own authority that he had conversations with Spinoza. In the whole history of philosophy there have been no unreported conversations which anyone interested in philosophy would have overheard with greater pleasure and profit. Nearly equal in intellectual stature and always concerned with the same fundamental problems, the two philosophers were utterly opposed in temperament and ambition, and in their conceptions of the philosopher's role in society. Leibniz, multifariously active and accessible, organizing, power-loving, avaricious, was a courtier and politician, a man of encyclopaedic knowledge and many attainments; he was immersed in the public life of his time at every point, writing and publishing incessantly on a great variety of subjects in response to some immediate need or request; he died miserable and unsatisfied, though indisputably the greatest intellect in Europe after Newton. By contrast Spinoza was inaccessible, secluded, unworldly, and self-sufficient; his whole life was narrowly concentrated in constructing a single metaphysical system and in drawing moral implications from it, and even his political writings were studiously remote from the actual details of current affairs. Leibniz, with his prodigies of technical invention, has posthumously remained in the main stream of European logic and science, while Spinoza has always been islanded and has left no legacy of logical invention.

Spinoza was consumptive, probably from an early age, and the glass dust from his lenses probably aggravated his condition. Having finished the *Ethics*, he spent the last years of his life on the *Political Treatise*, which he intended to be a more popular exposition of the principles of tolerance and of public order in a rational society; but he did not live to finish it. He died at the age of forty-four, peacefully and without public notice. He had arranged that his manuscripts should be placed in the hands of his philosophical friends, who immediately began to prepare them for anonymous publication, under title of *Opera Posthuma*, by B. D. S. The early work, called a *Short Treatise on God, Man and his Well-being*, was not discovered until nearly a hundred years later, and two essays, *The Calculation of Chances*, and *The Rainbow*, were also discovered later. His posthumous works, including the *Ethics*, were at first received with incomprehension and perfunctory abuse, and were generally neglected until the end of the eighteenth century.

He had the reputation of being a man of great courtesy and amenity, and among his neighbours he seems to have been loved and respected; he was certainly not dour, dull or disapproving. But he thought it right that a philosopher should remain impassively concealed behind his philosophy, and, like his intellectual ancestors, Euclid and Lucretius, he has effectively concealed himself behind his work.

Index of Subjects and Terms

Acquiescentia Animi, 121
Active *v.* Passive Emotions, 135–6
Adequacy (of Ideas), 87–107
Affectus, 135–6
Alexander, S., 196
Appetitus, 127
Aristotelian Logic, 33, 148
Aristotle, 175, 191
Association of Ideas, 90–3, 115, 134
Auxilia Imaginationis, 174

Bacon, 73, 229
Bayle, dictionary, 27
Beatitudo, 166
Bible, interpretation of, 203, 206–7, 229
Body and Mind, 58–69, 82–4, 127–34

Cause, 30, 34–54
    Causa Sui, 36–53
    First Cause, 44, 213–14, 216–17
    Ground, 136
    Immanent and Transient, 42–4
    Occasion, 63
Characteristica Universalis, 21
Clear and Distinct Ideas, 17–20, 23, 87–107
Cogito, Ergo Sum, 98–9
Cognitio Reflexiva, 97–9, 109–10
Common Notions, 95–6
Composite Images, 91–3, 116, 146
Conatus, 122–3, 127, 133, 138, 141–3

Contingent *v.* Necessary, 36–8
Convenientia, 87
Corpora Simplicissima, 72, 121
Creation, 40–5, 46, 51–4, 213–14
Cupiditas, 127

Decretum (Decision), 128
Descartes, 14, 16–18, 20–4, 38, 58–62, 66, 70–83, 86, 90, 91, 98–100, 104–6, 111, 117, 131, 132, 140, 196, 229–31
Determinism, 45, 107, 149–61
Deus sive natura, 39–45, 48–54, 168–71

Error, 106–7
Essence, 50, 51, 53–4, 76–7
Eternity, 43, 56, 171–6
Euclid, 17, 25, 46, 235
Experientia Vaga, 84–5, 152
Extension, 58–65, 69–81

Facies Totius Universi, 74
Fluctuatio Animi, 153
Fortitudo, 167
Freedom,
    as a citizen, 181–3, 186–8, 197–200
    free man, 125–7, 161–8
    of God, 44–6, 49–50, 51–3
    of the will, 149–61
    of thought, 197–201
Freud, 141–4

Index

Generositas, 167
Geometrical Method, 24–5

Happiness, 161–8
Hobbes, 91, 122, 177, 179–83
Hume, 212, 215, 226

Idea, 83–107
  Ideatum, of, 83–115, 123–9
Imagination, 18–24, 40, 82–94
Infinita Idea Dei, 89, 126
Infinite, 38–9, 56–8
Infinite Intellect of God, 83
Intellectual Love of God, 168–71

Joachim, H. H., 101

Kant, 212, 215, 226
Knowledge, levels of, 85–96, 103

Laetitia, 124, 162
Leibniz, 14, 21, 34, 52, 219, 233
Libido, 141–4
Lucretius, 169, 235

Machiavelli, 190
Maimonides, 207
Mathematics, paradigm of knowledge, 16–18, 95–6, 194–6, 220
Matter, 69–81, 212
Memory, 91
Metaphysics, nature of, 12–16, 32–3, 47–8, 71–2, 79–81, 210–26
Method, 97–9, 109–10, 114, 117–20
Mind, 58–9, 64–5, 68–9, 82–6

Modes, Finite and infinite, 69–76, 82–4, 89, 121–7
Montesquieu, 192
Motion and Rest, 70–2

Natura Naturans, Natura Naturata, 46, 54
Natural Light, 17
Newton, 14, 43
Nominalism, 91–5, 116–17, 138

Particular Things, 72–9
Perception, 84–90
Plato, 85, 117, 219, 226
Pleasure and Pain, 124, 127, 133–5, 162

Ratio, 94–6
Right, 180–7

Scientia Intuitiva, 103–4
Substance, 31–9, 62–5

Time, 43, 56, 171–6, 193–7
Titillatio, 162
Toleration, 178, 198–209
Truth, 86–90, 97–107, 117–20

Universal Notions, 92–3, 95, 146
Universe, 213–16

Vico, 27, 192

Will, 128–9, 149–54
Wittgenstein, 226
Words, 93

MORE ABOUT PENGUINS
AND PELICANS

AN INQUIRY INTO MEANING
AND TRUTH

Bertrand Russell

'It all depends what you mean by ...' The late Professor
C. E. M. Joad sometimes amused and sometimes irritated
listeners to the Brains Trust with this invariable comment on
the questions asked. But he was merely in accord with the
modern trend of philosophy, which nowadays stresses the importance of close linguistic analysis.

In this fundamental inquiry Bertrand Russell, author of *A
History of Western Philosophy* and probably the best-known
philosopher of our time, is concerned above all with language,
as he examines the processes of thought, expression, and knowledge with mathematical precision. What is the relation between
a belief and a sentence in which that belief is expressed? How
are we to set about defining 'knowledge' and 'truth' and relating
these concepts to our own experience?

In answering such questions Bertrand Russell applies the
methods of psychology as well as logic. Whilst his answers are
often complex – as, for precision, they must be – his arguments
are at all times both lucid and elegant.